MANUAL OF INDULGENCES

Manual of Indulgences

NORMS AND GRANTS

Apostolic Penitentiary

Translated into English from the fourth edition (1999)
of *Enchiridion Indulgentiarum:*
Normae et Concessiones

UNITED STATES CONFERENCE OF CATHOLIC BISHOPS
Washington, D.C.

Concordat cum originali:
    Msgr. James Patrick Moroney
    Executive Director, Secretariat for the Liturgy
    United States Conference of Catholic Bishops

ISBN: 978-1-57455-474-8

First printing, October 2006
Third printing, July 2013

CONTENTS

ABBREVIATIONS

AA	SECOND VATICAN COUNCIL, Decree *Apostolicam actuositatem* (*Decree on the Apostolate of Lay People*), November 18, 1965 (AAS 58 [1966] 837-864)
AAS	*Acta Apostolicae Sedis, Commentarium officiale*
AG	SECOND VATICAN COUNCIL, Decree *Ad gentes* (*Decree on the Church's Missionary Activity*), December 7, 1965 (AAS 58 [1966] 947-990)
AP	POPE BENEDICT XV, Motu proprio *Alloquentes proxime*, March 25, 1917 (AAS 9 [1917] 167)
Ap.	apostolic
can./cann.	canon/canons
CCC	*Catechismus Catholicae Ecclesiae* (*Catechism of the Catholic Church*), August 15, 1997
CD	SECOND VATICAN COUNCIL, Decree *Christus Dominus* (*Decree on the Pastoral Office of the Bishops in the Church*), October 28, 1965 (AAS 58 [1966] 673-701)
CE	*Caeremoniale Episcoporum* (*Ceremonial of Bishops*), September 14, 1984
CIC 1917	*Codex Iuris Canonici* (*Code of Canon Law*), May 27, 1917
CIC 1983	*Codex Iuris Canonici* (*Code of Canon Law*), January 25, 1983
conc.	concession/concessions
Const.	constitution
CS	POPE PIUS XII, Motu proprio *Cleri sanctitati*, June 2, 1957 (AAS 49 [1957] 433-600)

De Ben.   ROMAN RITUAL, *De benedictionibus* (*Book of Blessings*), May 31, 1984

Decl.   declaration

Decr.   decree

DH   SECOND VATICAN COUNCIL, Declaration *Dignitatis humanae* (*Declaration on Religious Liberty*), December 1965 (AAS 58 [1966] 929-946)

DS   DENZINGER-SCHÖNMETZER, *Enchiridion Symbolorum Definitionum et Declarationum de rebus fidei et morum*, ed. 33, 1965

EI 1968   *Enchiridion indulgentiarum: Normae et concessiones* (*Enchiridion of Indulgences: Norms and Concessions*), June 29, 1968

EI 1986   *Enchiridion indulgentiarum: Normae et concessiones* (*Enchiridion of Indulgences: Norms and Concessions*), May 18, 1986

gen.   general

GS   SECOND VATICAN COUNCIL, Pastoral Constitution *Gaudium et spes* (*Pastoral Constitution on the Church in the Modern World*), December 7, 1966 (AAS 58 [1966] 1025-1120)

ID   POPE PAUL VI, Apostolic Constitution *Indulgentiarum doctrina* (On Indulgences), January 1, 1967 (AAS 59 [1967] 5-24)

IFI   SACRED APOSTOLIC PENITENTIARY, Decree *In fere innumeris*, July 20, 1942 (AAS 34 [1942] 240)

LG   SECOND VATICAN COUNCIL, Dogmatic Constitution *Lumen gentium* (*Dogmatic Constitution on the Church*), November 21, 1964 (AAS 57 [1965] 5-71)

LH	*Liturgia Horarum* (*Liturgy of the Hours*), April 7, 1985
RM	*Roman Missal* (*Missale Romanum*), March 27, 1975
n./nn.	norm/norms
OT	SECOND VATICAN COUNCIL, Decree *Optatam totius* (*Decree on the Training of Priests*), October 28, 1965 (AAS 58 [1966] 713-727)
PA	Apostolic Penitentiary
Paen.	POPE PAUL VI, Apostolic Constitution *Paenitemini*, February 17, 1966 (AAS 58 [1966] 177-198)
PB	POPE JOHN PAUL II, Apostolic Constitution *Pastor bonus*, June 28, 1988 (AAS 80 [1988] 841-912)
PL	MIGNE, J.-P., ed., *Patrologia latina*, 1844-1855
Resp.	Response
REU	POPE PAUL VI, Apostolic Constitution *Regimini Ecclesiae Universae*, August 15 1967 (AAS 59 [1967] 885-928)
SC	SECOND VATICAN COUNCIL, Constitution *Sacrosanctum Concilium* (*Constitution on the Sacred Liturgy*), December 4, 1963 (AAS 56 [1964] 97-138)
SCR	Sacred Congregation of Rites
SPA	Sacred Apostolic Penitentiary
tab.	table
Vg	Vulgate

Foreword

"For it was from the side of Christ as He slept the sleep of death upon the cross that there came forth 'the wondrous sacrament of the whole Church'" (*Sacrosanctum Concilium*, no. 5). Through the merits of Christ's life, death, and resurrection, the whole of his body, the Church, benefits from the redemption which he has won for all. Intimately connected with the Sacrament of Penance, indulgences are given by the Church from her spiritual treasury to remit temporal punishment for sin. Thus, this *Manual of Indulgences* opens a special door to this treasury for all the faithful.

Indulgences are, in the words of Pope John Paul II, "the expression of the Church's full confidence of being heard by the Father when—in view of Christ's merits and, by his gift, those of Our Lady and the saints—she asks him to mitigate or cancel the painful aspect of punishment by fostering its medicinal aspect through other channels of grace" (Pope John Paul II, General Audience, September 29, 1999).

At the request of His Eminence, Cardinal William Wakefield Baum, then-Major Penitentiary of the Apostolic Penitentiary, the USCCB Secretariat for the Liturgy has produced this English language translation in collaboration with the Holy See. Just as with the previous edition of the *Manual of Indulgences*, the United States Conference of Catholic Bishops has gladly responded to the Holy See's request for assistance in providing an English-language edition of the *Enchiridion Indulgentiarum* to the English-speaking world.

May this present volume serve as an encouragement to all the faithful who stand in need of God's mercy.

Bishop William S. Skylstad
Bishop of Spokane
President,
United States Conference of Catholic Bishops

April 23, 2006
The Second Sunday of Easter
Divine Mercy Sunday

Manual of Indulgences

NORMS AND GRANTS

APOSTOLIC PENITENTIARY

Prot. N. 122/01/I

Decree

Pursuant to the request of His Excellency, The Most Reverend William Stephen Skylstad, Bishop of Spokane and President of the United States Conference of Bishops, by virtue of the faculties granted to this Dicastery by the Supreme Pontiff Benedict XVI, the Apostolic Penitentiary gladly approves the English translation of the fourth "editio typica" of the **Handbook of Indulgences**, insofar as it conforms to the amended original, and authorizes that it may lawfully published.

Inserted into said document must be the text of this entire Decree.

Moreover, two printed copies of the same publication are to be kindly forwarded to the Apostolic Penitentiary.

Anything to the contrary notwithstanding.

Given at Rome, from the Office of the Apostolic Penitentiary, October 12, 2005.

James Francis Stafford,
Cardinal of the Holy Roman Church
Major Penitentiary

Gianfranco Girotti, O.F.M.Conv.
Regent

Enchiridion Indulgentiarum, fourth edition (1999)

The infinitely precious merits of Jesus, Divine Redeemer of the human race, and their abundant progeny, the merits of the Blessed Virgin Mary and all the saints, have been entrusted to Christ's Church as an unfailing treasury, that they may be applied to the remission of sins and of the consequences of sin, by virtue of the power of binding and loosing which the Founder of the Church himself conferred on Peter and the other Apostles, and through them on their successors, the Supreme Pontiffs and Bishops. This remission is given primarily, and in the case of mortal sins necessarily, through the Sacrament of Reconciliation.

However, even after mortal sin has been forgiven and, as a necessary consequence, the eternal punishment it deserves has been remitted, and even if slight or venial sin has been remitted, the forgiven sinner can need further purification, that is, be deserving of temporal punishment to be expiated in this life or in the life to come, namely, in Purgatory. An indulgence, whose purpose is to remit this punishment, is drawn from the Church's wonderful treasury mentioned above. The doctrine of faith regarding indulgences and the praiseworthy practice of gaining them confirm and apply, with special efficacy for attaining holiness, the deeply consoling mysteries of the Mystical Body of Christ and the Communion of Saints.

The Supreme Pontiff John Paul II clearly explained all these points in the Bull of Indiction of the Great Jubilee *Incarnationis mysterium*.

In accordance with this act of the Magisterium, the Apostolic Penitentiary takes the opportunity offered by the now imminent opening of the sacred Jubilee and by the dissemination throughout the Catholic world of the above-mentioned Bull to republish—for the fourth time—the *Enchiridion Indulgentiarum*, in the form of the typical edition of June 29, 1968, which contains the disciplinary changes introduced by the Apostolic Constitution *Indulgentiarum doctrina*.

The principles governing indulgences have not been changed at all in this new edition, but several norms have been revised in the light of documents recently published by the Apostolic See.

Moreover, the grants are arranged systematically in such a way that their number is not really reduced even though the list is shorter. The method followed in indicating the grants was chosen in order to increase the devotion of supernatural charity in the individual members of the faithful and in the ecclesial community.

So, first of all, a fourth general grant was added, by which a public witness of faith, in the particular circumstances of everyday life, is enriched with an indulgence. The other new grants of particular importance concern the strengthening of the foundations of the Christian family (consecration of families); communion in the prayer of the universal Church (through active participation in days universally appointed for specific religious purposes and during the Week of Prayer for Christian Unity); and the worship to be given Jesus really present in the Blessed Sacrament (Eucharistic procession).

Several earlier grants have also been broadened, for example, regarding the recitation of the Marian Rosary or the Akathistos hymn, the jubilee celebrations of sacred ordinations, the reading of Sacred Scripture, and visits to sacred places.

This edition of the *Enchiridion* makes frequent reference to faculties granted to various episcopal assemblies (those of the Eastern Churches according to their respective juridical norms, those of the Latin rite according to canon 447 CIC, to prepare lists of prayers more commonly used in their respective territories). And, in fact, there has been a notable increase in the number of prayers included in the *Enchiridion*, especially those from the Eastern traditions.

By the present Decree the attached text is declared authentic and its publication is ordered by the authority of the Supreme Pontiff, as indicated in the Audience granted on July 5, 1999, to the Superiors of the Apostolic Penitentiary.

In accord with the intentions of the Holy Father, the Apostolic Penitentiary hopes that the faithful, prompted by the teaching and pastoral concern of their Bishops, will make use of sacred indulgences with heartfelt devotion to increase their piety, for the greater glory of the Divine and Most High Trinity.

Anything to the contrary notwithstanding.

Given in Rome, at the office of the Apostolic Penitentiary, July 16, 1999, the memorial of Our Lady of Mount Carmel.

Cardinal William Wakefield Baum
Major Penitentiary

+ Luigi De Magistris
Titular Bishop of Nova
Regent

INTRODUCTION

1. The publication of the first edition of this *Manual of Indulgences* in June 1968 was accomplished in fulfillment of norm 13 of the Apostolic Constitution *Indulgentiarum doctrina*, which laid down that "the *Manual of Indulgences* is to be revised in such a way that only the principal prayers and principal works of piety, charity and penance have an indulgence attached to them." In subsequent editions, including the present one, the Apostolic Penitentiary has taken care to make the text clearer, to correct some minor details in conformity with scholarly protocols, and to make some additions.

2. In this regard the principal prayers and principal works have been taken to be those which by tradition and by their suitability for present-day needs seem particularly apt, so that not only are faithful helped to make satisfaction for the punishment due their sins, but also, and above all, are encouraged to a greater zeal for the exercise of charity. This is the principle upon which the compilation of this work is based.[1]

3. In accordance with tradition, participation in the Sacrifice of the Mass or the Sacraments is not enriched by indulgences, by reason of the surpassing efficacy for "sanctification and purification" that they have in themselves.[2]

---

1 POPE PAUL VI, Address to the College of Cardinals and the Roman Curia, December 23, 1966 (AAS 59 [1967] 57).
2 Cf. ID, no. 11.

When an indulgence is granted for reason of a particular occasion (such as First Holy Communion, the celebration of his first Mass by a newly ordained priest, Mass at the conclusion of a Eucharistic Congress), the indulgence is not attached to participation in Mass or the Sacraments, but to the special occasion connected with such participation. The purpose of the indulgence is to promote and, as it were, reward the effort of commitment that is part of any festivity, the good done to other people, the good example shown, and the honor accorded the most Holy Eucharist and the Priesthood.

Nevertheless an indulgence can be attached, according to tradition, to various works of piety, both private and public; likewise, works of charity and penance, which in our own times are accorded increased importance, can also be so enriched. Yet all these works to which indulgences are attached, as indeed any good deed performed or any suffering patiently endured, are by no means separated from the Mass and the Sacraments. These, on the contrary, are the principal fonts of sanctification and purification,[3] since good works and sufferings are made into an oblation in which the faithful themselves are offered up, an oblation conjoined to the offering of Christ in the Eucharistic Sacrifice.[4] Similarly, the Mass and the Sacraments move the faithful to carry out their duties so that "by the manner of their life they hold fast to what they have received in faith,"[5] and these duties, in turn, when diligently carried out, make them day by day better disposed for fruitful participation in the Mass and the Sacraments.[6]

---

3 ID, no. 11.
4 Cf. LG, no. 34.
5 RM, Collect of Monday within the Octave of Easter.
6 Cf. SC, no. 9-13.

4. Regarding personal piety, increased emphasis is given to the act of the individual believer (*opus operantis*), whence long lists of pious works (*opus operatum*), as it were distinct from the daily life of the Christian, are not compiled. Rather, a relatively small number of grants is indicated,[7] the better to move the believer to make his life more fruitful and more holy, thereby eliminating "that split between the faith professed and the daily lives of many . . . by gathering into one vital synthesis all their undertakings in the human, domestic, professional, scholarly or technical sphere with religious values, under whose supreme direction all things are harmonized unto God's glory."[8]

The Apostolic Penitentiary therefore, rather than stress the repetition of formulas and acts, has been concerned to put greater emphasis on the Christian way of life and to focus attention on cultivating a spirit of prayer and penance and on the exercise of the theological virtues.

5. In the *Manual*, before various grants of indulgences are set out, the Norms are given, drawn principally from the Apostolic Constitution *Indulgentiarum doctrina* and the *Code of Canon Law*, and from other directives as well. To avoid any uncertainties that might arise about these matters, it was deemed opportune to provide an orderly and comprehensive exposition of all the directives currently in force regarding indulgences.

6. In the *Manual*, four grants of a more general nature are first presented, which may in some sense serve as beacons for the conduct of daily Christian life. For the benefit and instruction of the faithful, each of these general grants is supplemented by

---

7   Cf. below especially norms I-IV.
8   Cf. GS, no. 43.

quotations that illustrate how the particular grants are in harmony with the spirit of the Gospel and the renewal begun by the Second Vatican Council.

7. There follows a listing of grants pertaining to certain works of religion. These, however, are few in number, since several works are covered by the general grants, and since in the case of prayers explicit mention is limited to those of universal appeal and character. For editions of the *Manual* in the different languages, the competent episcopal conferences should take care to include, as appropriate, other prayers traditionally cherished and beneficial to the piety of the faithful.

8. The *Manual* contains an appendix giving a list of invocations along with the text of the Apostolic Constitution *Indulgentiarum doctrina*.

NORMS ON INDULGENCES

NORMS ON INDULGENCES*

N1. An indulgence is a remission before God of the temporal punishment for sins, whose guilt is forgiven, which a properly disposed member of the Christian faithful obtains under certain and clearly defined conditions through the intervention of the Church, which, as the minister of Redemption, dispenses and applies authoritatively the treasury of the expiatory works of Christ and the saints.

N2. An indulgence is partial or plenary according to whether it removes either part or all of the temporal punishment due sin.

N3. The faithful can obtain partial or plenary indulgences for themselves, or they can apply them to the dead by way of suffrage.

N4. The faithful who perform with at least inward contrition an action to which a partial indulgence is attached obtain, in addition to the remission of temporal punishment acquired by the action itself, an equal remission of punishment through the intervention of the Church.

---

*   Notes in this section are numbered by norm (and by sub-norm, as applicable).
1   CIC 1917, can. 911; ID, norm 1; EI 1968, norm 1; CIC 1983, can. 992; EI 1986, norm 1.
2   ID, norm 2; EI 1968, norm 2; CIC 1983, can. 993; EI 1986, norm 2.
3   CIC 1917, can. 930; ID, norm 3, EI 1968, norms 3-4; CIC 1983, can. 994; EI 1986, norms 3-4.
4   ID, norm 5; EI 1968, norm 6; EI 1986, norm 5.

N5.   §1. Besides the supreme authority of the Church, indulgences can be granted only by those to whom this power has been given by law or granted by the Roman Pontiff.

§2. No authority less than the Roman Pontiff can concede to others the power to grant indulgences unless it has been expressly granted by the Apostolic See.

N6.   In the Roman Curia, whatever pertains to the granting and use of indulgences is the competence of the Apostolic Penitentiary, always respecting the right of the Congregation for the Doctrine of the Faith to examine whatever pertains to dogmatic teaching concerning indulgences.

N7.   Eparchial and diocesan bishops, and others equivalent to them in law even if they lack episcopal rank, have the right from entrance upon their pastoral office:

    1. to grant within the territory of their jurisdiction a partial indulgence to all the faithful, and to those faithful belonging to their jurisdiction in places outside this territory.

    2. to impart in their respective eparchies or dioceses, according to the prescribed formula, the Papal Blessing with a plenary indulgence three times a year on solemn feasts which they have designated, even if they only assist at the Mass.

---

5   *§1:* CIC 1917, can. 912; EI 1968, norm 8; CIC 1983, can. 995 §1; EI 1986, norm 7.

     §2: CIC 1917, can. 913; EI 1968, norm 10, 1°: CIC 1983, can. 995 §2; EI 1986, norm 9.

6   AP, nos. 4-5; REU, no. 113; EI 1968, norm 9; EI 1986, norm 8; PB, no. 120.

7   *1°:* CIC 1917, can. 349 §2, 2°; IFI, no. 1; CS, cann. 396 §2, 2°, 364 §3, 3°, 367 §2, 1°, 391; EI 1968, norm 11 §1; EI 1986, norm 10, 1°.

     2°: CIC 1917, can. 914; IFI, I; EI 1968, norm 11 §2; CE, nos. 1122-1126; EI 1986, norm 10, 2°.

This Blessing is to be given at the conclusion of Mass in place of the customary blessing, according to the norms given in the *Ceremonial of Bishops*.

N8.   Metropolitans can grant a partial indulgence in either eparchial or suffragan dioceses, as if in their own territory.

N9.   §1. Patriarchs can grant the following in every place, even those exempt, of their own patriarchates; in churches of their rite outside the boundaries of their patriarchate; as well as to the faithful of their rite everywhere:

1. a partial indulgence
2. the Papal Blessing with a plenary indulgence three times a year according to ordinary law and whenever a plenary indulgence is warranted for the good of the faithful because of a particular religious circumstance or reason

§2. Major archbishops have the same faculty.

N10.   Cardinals of the Holy Roman Church have the faculty to grant a partial indulgence everywhere, but only to those present, and for that time only.

N11.   §1. The express permission of the Apostolic See is required to publish the *Enchiridion Indulgentiarum* in any language.

---

8   CIC 1917, can. 274, 2°; IFI, no. 2; CS, cann. 319, 6°, 320 §1, 4°; EI 1968, norm 12; EI 1986, norm 11.
9   *§1, 1°*: CS, can. 283, 4°; EI 1968, norm 13; EI 1986, norm 12.
       §2: CS, can. 326 §1, 10°; EI 1968, norm 13; EI 1968, norm 12.
10   CIC 1917, can. 239 §1, 24°; CS, can. 185 §1, 24°; EI 1968, norm 14; EI 1986, norm 13.
11   *§1*: CIC 1917, can. 1388 §2; EI 1968, norm 15 §2; EI 1986, norm 14 §2.

§2. No books, leaflets, and the like, which contain grants of indulgences, may be published without the permission of the local ordinary or hierarch.

N12. According to the mind of the Sovereign Pontiff grants of indulgences for all the faithful take effect only after authentic copies of these grants have been examined by the Apostolic Penitentiary.

N13. If a liturgical celebration or its external solemnity is lawfully transferred, it is understood that an indulgence attached to that liturgical celebration is likewise transferred to the same day.

N14. If a visit to a Church or an oratory is required to obtain an indulgence attached to a particular day, this may be accomplished from noon of the preceding day until midnight of the particular day.

N15. The faithful can acquire an indulgence if they use devoutly one of the following properly blessed pious objects, namely: a crucifix or cross, rosary, scapular, or medal.

N16. §1. Indulgences attached to visiting a church or oratory do not cease if the church is totally destroyed and then rebuilt within fifty years in the same or almost the same place and under the same title.

11   §2: CIC 1917, can. 1388 §1; EI 1968, norm 15 §1; CIC 1983, can. 826 §3; EI
       1986, norm 14 §1.
12   CIC 1917, can. 920; EI 1968, norm 16; EI 1986, norm 15.
13   CIC 1917, can. 922; EI 1968, norm 17; EI 1986, norm 16.
14   CIC 1917, can. 923; EI 1968, norm 18; EI 1986, norm 17.
15   ID, norm 17; EI 1968, norm 19; EI 1986, norm 18.
16   §l: CIC 1917, can. 924 §1 and can. 75; EI 1968, norm 20 §l; CIC 1983, can.
       78 §3; EI 1986, norm 19 §1.

§2. An indulgence attached to the use of an article of devotion ceases only if the article is destroyed or sold.

N17. §1. In order to be capable of gaining indulgences one must be baptized, not excommunicated, and in the state of grace at least at the completion of the prescribed works.

§2. To gain an indulgence, one must have at least the general intention of doing so and must carry out the enjoined works at the stated time and in due fashion, according to the sense of the grant.

N18. §1. A plenary indulgence can be acquired only once in the course of a day; a partial indulgence can be acquired multiple times.

§2. The faithful however can obtain the plenary indulgence *at the hour of death*, even if they have already gained one on the same day.

N19. The work prescribed for acquiring a plenary indulgence connected with a church or oratory consists of a devout visit during which an Our Father and the Creed are recited, unless other directives have been laid down.

---

16 *§2:* CIC 1917, can. 924 §2 and can. 75; EI 1968, norm 20 §2; CIC 1983, can. 78 §3; EI 1986, norm 19 §2.

17 *§1:* CIC 1917, can. 925 §1; EI 1968, norm 22 §1; CIC 1983, can. 996 §1; EI 1986, norm 20 §1.
§2: CIC 1917, can. 925 §2; EI 1968, norm 22 §2; CIC 1983, can. 996 §2; EI 1986, norm 20 §2.

18 *§1:* CIC 1917, can. 928; ID, norm 6; EI 1968, norm 24 §§1, 3; EI 1986, norm 21 §§1, 3.
§2: ID, norm 18; EI 1968, norm 24 §2; EI 1986, norm 21 §2.

19 ID, norm 16; EI 1968, norm 25; EI 1986, norm 22.

20 *§1:* ID, norm 7; EI 1968, norm 26; EI 1986, norm 23 §1.

N20. §1. To gain a plenary indulgence, in addition to excluding all attachment to sin, even venial sin, it is necessary to perform the indulgenced work and fulfill the following three conditions: sacramental confession, Eucharistic Communion, and prayer for the intention of the Sovereign Pontiff.

§2. A single sacramental confession suffices for gaining several plenary indulgences; but Holy Communion must be received and prayer for the intention of the Holy Father must be recited for the gaining of each plenary indulgence.

§3. The three conditions may be fulfilled several days before or after the performance of the prescribed work; it is, however, fitting that Communion be received and the prayer for the intention of the Holy Father be said on the same day the work is performed.

§4. If the full disposition is lacking, or if the work and the three prescribed conditions are not fulfilled, saving the provisions given in Norm 24 and in Norm 25 regarding those who are "impeded," the indulgence will only be partial.

§5. The condition of praying for the intention of the Holy Father is fully satisfied by reciting one Our Father and one Hail Mary; nevertheless, one has the option of reciting any other prayer according to individual piety and devotion, if recited for this intention.

N21. §1. Unless otherwise stated, an indulgence cannot be gained by a work already imposed by law or precept.

---

20 §2: ID, norm 9; EI 1968, norm 28; EI 1986, norm 23 §2.
   §3: ID, norm, 8; EI 1968, norm 27; EI 1986, norm 23 §3.
   §4: ID, norm 7, in fine; EI 1968, norm 26, in fine; EI 1986, norm 23 §4.
   §5: ID, norm 10; EI 1968, norm 29; EI 1986, norm 23 §5.
21 §1: CIC 1917, can. 932; EI 1968, norm 31; EI 1986, norm 24.
   §2: CIC 1917, can. 932; EI 1968, norm 31; EI 1986, norm 24.

§2. One, however, who performs a work which has been imposed as a sacramental penance and which happens to be one enriched with an indulgence, can at the same time both satisfy the penance and gain the indulgence.

§3. Similarly, members of institutes of consecrated life and societies of the apostolic life can obtain the indulgences attached to prayers and pious works already obligatory by reason of their rules and constitutions or by precept.

N22. An indulgence attached to a prayer can be acquired by reciting the prayer in any language, provided that the translation is approved by the competent ecclesiastical authority.

N23. To gain an indulgence it is sufficient to recite the prayer alternately with a companion or to follow it mentally while it is being recited by another.

N24. Confessors can commute either the prescribed work or the conditions in favor of those for whom these are impossible because of a legitimate impediment.

N25. Hierarchs or local ordinaries can grant permission to the faithful over whom they exercise legitimate authority and who live in places where it is impossible or at least very difficult to go to confession or Communion to gain a plenary indulgence without confession and Communion, provided they have contrition for their sins and have the intention of receiving these Sacraments as soon as possible.

---

21 §3: PA, *Responsio ad propositum dubium*, July 1, 1992 (AAS 84 [1992] 935).
22 CIC 1917, can. 934 §2; EI 1968, norm 32; EI 1986, norm 25.
23 CIC 1917, can. 934 §3; EI 1968, norm 33; EI 1986, norm 26.
24 CIC 1917, can. 935; EI 1968, norm 34; EI 1986, norm 27.
25 ID, norm 11; EI 1968, norm 35; EI 1986, norm 28.

N26. Both the deaf and the mute can gain indulgences attached to public prayers if, together with the other faithful praying in the same place, they devoutly raise their mind and affections to God; regarding private prayers it is sufficient for them to recite the prayers mentally or express them with signs, or simply to read them without pronouncing the words.

---

26   CIC 1917, can. 936; EI 1968, norm 36: EI 1986, norm 29.

THE FOUR
GENERAL
CONCESSIONS

Introduction

1. Presented in the first place are the four general concessions by which the Christian faithful are encouraged to infuse with a Christian spirit[1] all the actions that go to make up their daily lives and to strive in the ordering of their lives toward the perfection of charity.[2]

2. These four grants are, in fact, very general, and each of them includes many works of the same type. Nevertheless, not all such works are endowed with indulgences, but only those which are carried out in a special manner and spirit.

Hence, by the first grant—which is as follows: "A partial indulgence is granted to the Christian faithful who, while carrying out their duties and enduring the hardships of life, raise their minds in humble trust to God and make, at least mentally, some pious invocation"—only those acts are indulgenced by means of which the Christian faithful raise up their mind to God, as stated, while performing their duties and bearing the hardships of life. Owing to human weakness, such special acts are not frequent.

Should someone be devout and zealous enough to fill the day with such acts, he would justly merit, over and above the increase of grace, a fuller remission of punishment, and he can bring in his charity more abundant aid to the souls in purgatory.

---

1   Cf. 1 Cor 10:31; Col 3:17; AA, nos. 2-4, 13.
2   Cf. LG, nos. 39, 40-42.

3. Since these four grants are fully in harmony with the Gospel and the doctrine of the Church, as clearly set forth by the Second Vatican Council, citations from Holy Scripture and the acts of this same Council are given below for each of the grants, for the benefit of the faithful.

The Grants

I

A partial indulgence is granted to the Christian faithful who, while carrying out their duties and enduring the hardships of life, raise their minds in humble trust to God and make, at least mentally, some pious invocation.[1]

By this first grant, the faithful are guided to fulfill the command of Christ, "Pray always without becoming weary,"[2] and at the same time are admonished to carry out their respective duties to preserve and strengthen their union with Christ.

Indeed, the mind of the Church in granting this indulgence is best illustrated by the following quotations taken from Sacred Scripture:

> "Ask and it will be given to you; seek and you will find; knock and the door will be opened to you. For everyone who asks, receives; and the one who seeks, finds; and to the one who knocks, the door will be opened."[3]
>
> "Watch and pray that you may not undergo the test."[4]
>
> "Beware that your hearts do not become drowsy from . . . the anxieties of daily life. . . . Be vigilant at all times and pray."[5]

---

1   Cf. SAP, Decr. *Pia oblatio quotidiani laboris Indulgentiis ditatur*, November 25, 1961 (AAS 53 [1961] 827); Decr. *Pia oblatio humani doloris Indulgentiis ditatur*, June 4, 1962 (AAS 54 [1962] 475); EI 1968 and 1986, gen. conc. I.

2   Lk 18:1.

3   Mt 7:7-8.

4   Mt 26:41.

5   Lk 21:34, 36.

"They were persevering, however, in the teaching and preaching of the apostles, in the breaking of the bread and in the prayers."[6]

"Rejoice in hope, be patient in trials, be constant in prayer."[7]

"Whether then you are eating or drinking, or whatever you are doing, do all for the glory of God."[8]

"With all prayer and supplication, pray at every opportunity in the Spirit. To that end, be watchful with all perseverance and supplication for all the holy ones."[9]

"And whatever you do, in word or in deed, do everything in the name of the Lord Jesus, giving thanks to God the Father through him."[10]

"Persevere in prayer, being watchful in it with thanksgiving."[11]

"Pray without ceasing. In all circumstances give thanks."[12]

And in the acts of Vatican Council II we read:

"All the faithful, therefore, whatever their condition of life, their duties or their circumstances, and through all of them, will grow daily in holiness if they accept all these things in faith from the hand of their heavenly Father and if they cooperate with the divine will by making manifest to all, even as they carry out their work here on earth, that love with which God has loved the world."[13]

---

6   Acts 2:42.
7   Rom 12:12.
8   1 Cor 10:31.
9   Eph 6:18.
10   Col 3:17.
11   Col 4:2.
12   1 Th 5:17-18.
13   LG, no. 41.

"This life of intimate union with Christ in the Church is nourished by spiritual aids common to all the faithful. . . . These aids should be so used that lay people, while duly carrying out their responsibilities in the world in the ordinary conditions of life, do not allow any separation of their union with Christ but rather grow in this union by doing their work according to God's will. . . . Neither providing for their families nor any other business in the secular world should be thought to be outside the scope of the spiritual life: as the apostle says, 'Whatever you do, in word or deed, do everything in the name of the Lord Jesus Christ, giving thanks to God the Father through him.'[14]"[15]

"The split between the faith which they profess and the daily lives of many people is to be counted as among the more serious misconceptions of our day. . . . No false opposition should be set up between professional and social activities on the one hand and the life of religion on the other. . . . On the contrary, Christians should rejoice that, following the example of Christ who worked as a craftsman, they are in a position to engage in all their earthly activities and they should bring their human, domestic, professional, scientific and technical activities into a living synthesis with religious values which orient and coordinate everything to the glory of God."[16]

14 Col 3:17.
15 AA, no. 4.
16 GS, no. 43.

II

A partial indulgence is granted to the faithful who, led by the spirit of faith, give compassionately of themselves or of their goods to serve their brothers in need.[17]

By the granting of this indulgence, the faithful are encouraged to perform more frequent works of charity and mercy, following the example and command of Jesus Christ.[18]

Nevertheless, not all works of charity are enriched with this indulgence, but only works that "serve their brothers in need"—such as those in want of food or clothing for the body or of instruction or comfort for the soul.

> "For I was hungry and you gave me food, I was thirsty and you gave me drink, a stranger and you welcomed me, naked and you clothed me, ill and in prison and you visited me. . . . Amen, I say to you, whatever you did for one of these least brothers of mine, you did for me."[19]

> "I give you a new commandment: love one another. As I have loved you, so you also should love one another. This is how all will know that you are my disciples, if you have love for one another."[20]

> "If one contributes, in generosity; if one does acts of mercy, with cheerfulness; love one another with mutual affection, anticipate one another in showing honor. Do not grow slack in zeal, be fervent in spirit,

---

17   Cf. SPA, *Indulgentiae apostolicae*, June 27, 1963 (AAS 55 [1963] 657-659); EI 1968 and 1986, gen. conc. II.

18   Cf. Jn 13:15; Acts 10:38.

19   Mt 25:35-36, 40; cf. also Tob 4:7-8; Is 58:7.

20   Jn 13:34-35.

serve the Lord. Contribute to the needs of the holy ones, exercise hospitality."[21]

"If I give away everything I own . . . but do not have love, I gain nothing."[22]

"So then, while we have the opportunity, let us do good to all, but especially to those who belong to the family of the faith."[23]

"Live in love, as Christ loved us."[24]

"You yourselves have been taught by God to love one another."[25]

"Let mutual love continue."[26]

"Religion that is pure and undefiled before God and the Father is this: to care for orphans and widows in their affliction and to keep oneself unstained by the world."[27]

"Since you have purified yourselves by obedience to the truth for sincere mutual love, love one another intensely from a pure heart."[28]

"Finally, all of you, be of one mind, sympathetic, loving toward one another, compassionate, humble. Do not return evil for evil, or insult for insult; but, on the contrary, a blessing, because to this you were called. That you might inherit a blessing."[29]

---

21 Rom 12:8, 10-11, 13.
22 1 Cor 13:3.
23 Gal 6:10.
24 Eph 5:2.
25 1 Th 4:9.
26 Heb 13:1.
27 Jas 1:27; cf. Jas 2:15-16.
28 1 Pt 1:22.
29 1 Pt 3:8-9.

"Make every effort to supplement . . . devotion with mutual affection, mutual affection with love."[30]

"If someone who has worldly means sees a brother in need and refuses him compassion, how can the love of God remain in him? Children, let us love not in word or speech but in deed and truth."[31]

"Wherever there are those who lack food and drink, clothes, a home, medicine, employment, education or whatever is needed for living a truly human life, those who suffer from hardship or ill health, exile or imprisonment, they should be sought out by Christian charity, supported by solicitous care and provided with practical aid . . . So that the exercise of charity may be manifestly above criticism, it is necessary to consider in our neighbor the image of God in which he was created, and Our Lord Christ to whom we offer whatever we give to one in need."[32]

"Since works of charity and mercy bear a most outstanding witness to the Christian life, apostolic formation should lead to the practice of these too, so that the faithful learn from early childhood to have compassion on their fellow human beings and generously help those in need."[33]

"Mindful of the Lord's words, 'thus all will know that you are my disciples, if you have love for one another,'[34] Christians can have nothing more at heart than to be of ever more generous service to humanity in the modern world. . . . The Father wishes us to recognize

30   2 Pt 1:5; 7.
31   1 Jn 3:17-18.
32   AA, no. 8.
33   AA, no. 31c.
34   Jn 13:35.

and extend active love in word and deed to Christ our brother in people everywhere. . . ."[35]

III

A partial indulgence is granted to the Christian faithful who, in a spirit of penance, voluntarily abstain from something that is licit for and pleasing to them.[36]

This grant is particularly suitable for our times in which, over and above the mild law regarding fast and abstinence, it is altogether opportune that the faithful be encouraged to practice penance.[37]

By holding their appetites in check, the faithful are moved to regain mastery of their bodies and to conform themselves to the poor and suffering Christ.[38]

Self-denial, however, will be more precious if it is joined to charity, in accord with the teaching of St. Leo the Great: "We should pay to good works what we refuse to indulgence. Let the poor man feast on what our fasting has denied us."[39]

> "If anyone wishes to come after me, he must deny himself and take up his cross daily and follow me."[40]
>
> "If you do not repent, you will all perish as they did."[41]

---

35 GS, no. 93.
36 EI 1968 and 1986, gen. conc. III.
37 Cf. Paen. III c.
38 Cf. Mt 8:20, 16:24.
39 *Sermo* 13 (alias: 12) *De ieiunio decimi mensis*, 2 (PL 54, 172).
40 Lk 9:23; cf. Lk 14:27.
41 Lk 13:5; cf. Lk 13:3.

"If by the Spirit you put to death the deeds of the body, you will live."[42]

"If only we suffer with him so that we may also be glorified with him."[43]

"Every athlete exercises discipline in every way. They do it to win a perishable crown, but we an imperishable one. Thus I do not run aimlessly; I do not fight as if I were shadowboxing. No. I drive my body and train it."[44]

"Always carrying about in the body the dying of Jesus, so that the life of Jesus may also be manifested in our body."[45]

"This saying is trustworthy: If we have died with him we shall also live with him; if we persevere we shall also reign with him."[46]

"[Rejecting] worldly desires [we should] live temperately, justly, and devoutly in this age."[47]

"But rejoice to the extent that you share in the sufferings of Christ, so that when his glory is revealed you may also rejoice exultantly."[48]

"With special care they should be so trained in priestly obedience, poverty and a spirit of self-denial, that they may accustom themselves to living in conformity with the crucified Christ and to giving up willingly even those things which are lawful."[49]

"The faithful indeed, by virtue of their royal priesthood, participate in the offering of the Eucharist. They

---

42   Rom 8:13.
43   Rom 8:17.
44   1 Cor 9:25-27.
45   2 Cor 4:10.
46   2 Tm 2:11-12.
47   Tt 2:12.
48   1 Pt 4:13.
49   OT, no. 9.

exercise that priesthood, too, by the reception of the sacraments, prayer and thanksgiving, the witness of a holy life, abnegation, and active charity."[50]

"The forms and tasks of life are many but holiness is one—that sanctity which is cultivated by all who act under God's Spirit and, obeying the Father's voice and adoring God the Father in spirit and truth, follow Christ, poor, humble and cross-bearing, that they may deserve to be partakers of his glory."[51]

"The Church nevertheless appeals to all the faithful together that they obey the Lord's command to repent not only through the hardships and setbacks bound up with the nature of daily life, but also by acts of bodily mortification. . . . The Church is intent especially upon expressing the three principal ways, longstanding in its practice, which make it possible to fulfill the divine command to repent. These are prayer, fasting, and works of charity—even though fast and abstinence have had a privileged place. These ways of penance have been shared by all the centuries; yet in our own time there are particular reasons advanced in favor of one way of penance above the others, depending on circumstances. For example, in the richer nations stress is placed on the witness of self-denial so that Christians will not become worldly; another emphasis is the witness of charity toward others, even those in foreign lands, who are suffering poverty and hunger."[52]

---

50   LG, no. 10.
51   LG, no. 41.
52   Paen. III c.

IV

A partial indulgence is granted to the Christian faithful who, in the particular circumstances of daily life, voluntarily give explicit witness to their faith before others.

This grant encourages the faithful to profess their faith openly before others, for the glory of God and the building up of the Church.

St. Augustine wrote: "Let your Creed be a mirror for you. See yourself in it, if you believe all that you profess, and rejoice daily in your faith."[53] The Christian life of each and every day, therefore, will be like the "Amen" concluding the "I believe" of our profession of baptismal faith.[54]

> "Everyone who acknowledges me before others I will acknowledge before my heavenly Father."[55]
>
> "Rather, blessed are those who hear the word of God and observe it."[56]
>
> "You will be my witnesses."[57]
>
> "Every day they devoted themselves to meeting together in the temple area and to breaking bread in their homes. They ate their meals with exultation and sincerity of heart, praising God and enjoying favor with all the people."[58]
>
> "The community of believers was of one heart and mind. . . . With great power the apostles bore witness to

---

53 *Sermo* 58, 11, 13 (PL 38:399).
54 Cf. CCC, no. 1064.
55 Mt 10:32.
56 Lk 11:28.
57 Acts 1:8.
58 Acts 2:46.

the resurrection of the Lord Jesus, and great favor was accorded them all."[59]

"Your faith is heralded throughout the world."[60]

"For, if you confess with your mouth that Jesus is Lord and believe in your heart that God raised him from the dead, you will be saved. For one believes with the heart and so is justified, and one confesses with the mouth and so is saved."[61]

"Compete well for the faith. Lay hold of eternal life, to which you were called when you made the noble confession in the presence of many witnesses."[62]

"So do not be ashamed of your testimony to our Lord."[63]

"But let no one among you be made to suffer as a murderer, a thief, an evildoer, or as an intriguer. But whoever is made to suffer as a Christian should be not ashamed but glorify God because of the name."[64]

"Whoever acknowledges that Jesus is the Son of God, God remains in him and he in God."[65]

"However, if charity is to grow in the soul like good seed and bear fruit, each individual believer must give the word of God a willing hearing and with the help of his grace do God's will, take part often in the sacraments, especially the Eucharist, and in the sacred liturgy. He should apply himself constantly to prayer, self-denial, active fraternal service and the practice of all the virtues."[66]

---

59 Acts 4:32-33.
60 Rom 1:8.
61 Rom 10:9-10.
62 1 Tm 6:12.
63 2 Tm 1:8.
64 1 Pt 4:15-16.
65 1 Jn 4:15.
66 LG, no. 42.

"The Christian faithful are called as individuals to exercise their apostolate in the various circumstances of their lives; but they should remember that human beings are by nature social. . . . Therefore, the faithful should exercise their apostolate in concert. Let them be as apostles in the community of their families and in parishes and dioceses, which express the communitarian nature of the apostolate, as well as in the free associations they decide to join."[67]

"The social nature of human beings, however, requires that they should express these interior religious acts externally, share their religion with others, and witness to it communally."[68]

"It is not sufficient, however, that the Christian people be present and established in a particular nation, nor is sufficient that they practice the apostolate of good example. The purpose for which they are established, the purpose for which they are present, is to proclaim Christ to their non-Christian fellow citizens by word and deed and to help them to receive Christ fully."[69]

---

67 AA, no. 18.
68 DH, no. 3.
69 AG, no. 15.

OTHER CONCESSIONS

Introduction

1. In addition to the four general grants (set forth under numbers I-IV above), several others are provided which, in consideration of the traditions of the past as well as the needs of our own time, are of particular importance.

All these grants complement one another and, while drawing the faithful by the gift of an indulgence to perform works of devotion, charity, and penance, lead them through charity to a more intimate union with Christ the Head and with the Church his Body.[1]

2. Certain other prayers, owing to their divine inspiration, or to their venerable antiquity and universal usage, are included herein[2] and cited, as is obvious, by way of example. That which is set forth in the norms regarding the rights of bishops, eparchs, metropolitans, patriarchs, and cardinals must, however, be borne in mind.[3]

The nature of prayer itself ensures that the faithful of any rite can acquire the indulgences granted for the pious recitation of prayers, lists of which are found below, whatever the liturgical tradition to which a particular prayer belongs.

3. If the matter is viewed more closely, these prayers can be understood as subsumed under the first general grant, when

---

1   Cf. ID, no. 11.
2   E.g., *Credo* (conc. 28 §2, 3°); *De profundis* (conc. 9, 2°); *Magnificat* (conc. 17 §2, 1°); *Sub tuum praesidium* (conc. 17 §2, 3°); *Salve, Regina* (ibid.); *Actiones nostras* (conc. 26 §2, 2°); *Agimus tibi gratias* (ibid.).
3   Cf. norms 7-10, 11 §2, 22, 25.

they are recited by the faithful in the course of their everyday lives, with their minds raised in humble trust to God. Some examples of the prayers included in the first grant are the *Actiones nostras* and the *Agimus tibi gratias*, which are recited in the course of "carrying out one's duties."

Nevertheless, it seemed helpful to list these prayers individually as endowed with indulgences in order to eliminate any doubt about them, and to demonstrate their excellence.

4. As is obvious, whenever the grant of an indulgence requires the recitation of prayers, litanies, or the little office, the text must always be approved by the competent ecclesiastical authority. Such recitation, as well as visits to sacred places, acts of piety, or use of a devotional object—when prescribed—must be performed devoutly and with interior reverence. For certain grants, this understanding is expressly noted to aid the piety of the faithful.

5. To obtain a plenary indulgence, as stated in Norm 20, the performance of the work, the fulfillment of the three conditions, and a generous disposition of heart, which would exclude all attachment to sin, are required.

The performance of the prescribed work and at least a contrite heart are required for a partial indulgence, as noted in Norm 4.

6. If the work to which a plenary indulgence is attached can be readily divided into parts (e.g., the decades of the Marian rosary), whoever, owing to some reasonable cause, cannot complete the entire work can obtain a partial indulgence for the part completed.[4]

---

4   Cf. norm 20 §4.

7. Deserving of special mention are grants pertaining to those works by any one of which the faithful can obtain a plenary indulgence each day of the year, always safeguarding Norm 18 §1, according to which a plenary indulgence can be acquired no more than once a day:

— adoration of the Blessed Sacrament for at least one half hour (grant 7 §1, 1°)

— the pious exercise of the Way of the Cross (grant 13, 2°)

— recitation of the Marian rosary or of the hymn *Akathistos*, in church or an oratory; or in a family, a religious community, or a sodality of the faithful or, in general, when several of the faithful are gathered for any good purpose (grant 17 §1, 1°, and grant 23 §1)

— the devout reading or listening to the Sacred Scriptures for at least a half an hour (grant 30)

8. The grants are listed in alphabetical order based on the first words of their titles in the original Latin text (e.g., *Actus consecrationis familiarum* [Act of Consecration of a Family], or *Eucharistica adoratio et processio* [Eucharistic Adoration and Procession]).

The sources from which these prayers have been taken are indicated only when excerpted from liturgical texts now in use.

To make the use of the *Manual* easier for the Christian faithful, three indices are added:

— the texts of prayers

— a list of times and acts by which a plenary indulgence is obtained

— a general index

Grants[*]

1

ACT OF FAMILY CONSECRATION

A *plenary indulgence* is granted to the members of the family on the day on which it is first consecrated, if at all possible by a priest or deacon, to the Most Sacred Heart of Jesus or to the Holy Family of Jesus, Mary, and Joseph, if they devoutly recite the duly approved prayer before an image of the Sacred Heart or the Holy Family; on the anniversary of the consecration, *the indulgence will be partial.*

2

ACT OF DEDICATION OF THE HUMAN RACE TO JESUS CHRIST THE KING

A *plenary indulgence* is granted to the faithful who on the solemnity of Our Lord Jesus Christ, King of the Universe, publicly recite the act of dedication of the human race to Christ the King (*Iesu dulcissime, Redemptor*); a *partial indulgence* is granted for its use in other circumstances.

---

*   Notes in this section are numbered by grant (and by sub-grant, as applicable).

2   EI 1986, conc. 17 (likewise in EI 1968).

Iesu dulcissime, Redemptor

Most sweet Jesus, Redeemer of the human race, look down upon us humbly prostrate before you. We are yours, and yours we wish to be; but to be more surely united with you, behold each one of us freely consecrates himself today to your Most Sacred Heart. Many indeed have never known you; many, too, despising your precepts, have rejected you. Have mercy on them all, most merciful Jesus, and draw them to your Sacred Heart. Be King, O Lord, not only of the faithful who have never forsaken you, but also of the prodigal children who have abandoned you; grant that they may quickly return to their Father's house, lest they die of wretchedness and hunger. Be King of those who are deceived by erroneous opinions, or whom discord keeps aloof, and call them back to the harbor of truth and the unity of faith, so that soon there may be but one flock and one Shepherd. Grant, O Lord, to your Church assurance of freedom and immunity from harm; give tranquility of order to all nations; make the earth resound from pole to pole with one cry: Praise to the divine Heart that wrought our salvation; to it be glory and honor for ever. Amen.

3

ACT OF REPARATION

A *plenary indulgence* is granted to the faithful who, on the solemnity of the Most Sacred Heart of Jesus, publicly recite the act of reparation (*Iesu dulcissime*); a *partial indulgence* is granted for its use in other circumstances.

Iesu dulcissime

Most sweet Jesus, whose overflowing charity for men is requited by so much forgetfulness, negligence, and contempt, behold us prostrate before you, eager to repair by a special act of homage the cruel indifference and injuries to which your loving Heart is everywhere subjected.

Mindful, alas! that we ourselves have had a share in such great indignities, which we now deplore from the depths of our hearts, we humbly ask your pardon and declare our readiness to atone by voluntary expiation, not only for our own personal offenses, but also for the sins of those who, straying far from the path of salvation, refuse in their obstinate infidelity to follow you, their Shepherd and Leader, or, renouncing the promises of their Baptism, have cast off the sweet yoke of your law.

We are now resolved to expiate each and every deplorable outrage committed against you;

---

3   EI 1986, conc. 26.

we are determined to make amends for the manifold offenses against Christian modesty in indecent dress and behavior, for all the foul seductions laid to ensnare the feet of the innocent, for the frequent violations of Sundays and holydays, and for the shocking blasphemies uttered against you and your Saints. We wish also to make amends for the insults to which your Vicar on earth and your priests are subjected, for the profanation, by conscious neglect or terrible acts of sacrilege, of the very Sacrament of your divine love, and lastly for the public crimes of nations who resist the rights and teaching authority of the Church which you have founded.

Would that we were able to wash away such abominations with our blood. We now offer, in reparation for these violations of your divine honor, the satisfaction you once made to your Eternal Father on the cross and which you continue to renew daily on our altars; we offer it in union with the acts of atonement of your Virgin Mother and all the saints and of the pious faithful on earth; and we sincerely promise to make recompense, as far as we can with the help of your grace, for all neglect of your great love and for the sins we and others have committed in the past. Henceforth, we will live a life of unswerving faith, of purity of conduct, of perfect observance of the precepts of the

Gospel and especially that of charity. We promise to the best of our power to prevent others from offending you and to bring as many as possible to follow you.

O loving Jesus, through the intercession of the Blessed Virgin Mother, our model in reparation, deign to receive the voluntary offering we make of this act of expiation; and by the crowning gift of perseverance keep us faithful unto death in our duty and the allegiance we owe to you, that we may all one day come to that happy home, where with the Father and the Holy Spirit you live and reign, for ever and ever. Amen.

4

PAPAL BLESSING

A *plenary indulgence* is granted to the faithful who devoutly receive a blessing imparted either by the Supreme Pontiff to Rome and the World (*Urbi et Orbi*), or by the bishop to whose care the faithful are entrusted in accordance with Norm 7, 2° of this *Manual*, even if, because of reasonable circumstances, they are unable to be present physically at the sacred rite, provided that they follow it devoutly as it is broadcast live by television or radio.

---

4   EI 1986, conc. 12 (cf. SPA, decr. *De indulgentiis ope instrumenti televisifici vel radiophonici lucrandis*, December 14, 1985: AAS 78 [1986] 293-294).

5

DAYS DESIGNATED UNIVERSALLY FOR A CERTAIN RELIGIOUS INTENTION

A *plenary indulgence* is granted to the faithful who, on days universally designated to foster certain religious intentions (e.g., the promotion of priestly and religious vocations, the pastoral care of the sick and infirm, strengthening the profession of faith in young people, and assisting others to lead a holy life, etc.), piously assist at celebrations of this kind; however, those who pray for these same intentions may gain a *partial indulgence*.

6

CHRISTIAN DOCTRINE

A *partial indulgence* is granted to the faithful who teach or study Christian doctrine.

7

EUCHARISTIC ADORATION AND PROCESSION

§1   A *plenary indulgence* is granted to the faithful who
   1° visit the Blessed Sacrament for adoration lasting at least a half hour;
   2° piously recite the verses of the *Tantum ergo* after the Mass of the Lord's Supper on Holy Thursday during the solemn reposition of the Most Blessed Sacrament;

---

5   Cf. EI 1986, conc. 37.
6   EI 1986, conc. 20 (the partial indulgence acquired by the teacher by reason of general concession II is extended by this grant to the one who studies).
7   *§1, 1°*: EI 1986, conc. 3.
   §1, 2°: EI 1986, conc. 59.

3° devoutly participate in a solemn Eucharistic procession, held inside or outside a church, of greatest importance on the Solemnity of the Body and Blood of Christ;

4° participate religiously in the solemn Eucharistic celebration which is customarily held at the conclusion of a Eucharistic congress.

§2 A *partial indulgence* is granted to the faithful who
1° visit the Blessed Sacrament for adoration;
2° offer any duly approved prayer to Jesus present in the Blessed Sacrament (e.g., the *Adoro te devote*, the prayer O *sacrum convivium*, or the *Tantum ergo*).

O sacrum convivium

O sacred banquet, in which Christ is received, the memory of his Passion is renewed, the mind is filled with grace, and a pledge of future glory is given to us.

Tantum ergo

Down in adoration falling,
Lo! the sacred Host we hail;
Lo! o'er ancient forms departing,
Newer rites of grace prevail;
Faith for all defects supplying,
Where the feeble senses fail.
To the everlasting Father,

---

7 §1, 4°: EI 1986, conc. 23.
  §2, 1°: EI 1986, conc. 3.
  §2, 2°: EI 1986, conc. 4, 40, 59.

And the Son who reigns on high,
With the Holy Spirit proceeding
Forth from each eternally,
Be salvation, honor, blessing,
Might and endless majesty. Amen.

V. You have given them bread from heaven,
R̶. Having all delight within it.

Let us pray. O God, who in this wonderful Sacrament left us a memorial of your Passion: grant, we implore you, that we may so venerate the sacred mysteries of your Body and Blood, as always to be conscious of the fruit of your Redemption. You who live and reign forever and ever. Amen.

(Holy Communion and Worship of the
Eucharist Outside of Mass;
June 21, 1973, nos. 200, 192)

8

EUCHARISTIC AND SPIRITUAL COMMUNION

§1   A *plenary indulgence* is granted to the faithful who
    1° receive Holy Communion for the first time or devoutly assist at the first Holy Communion of others;
    2° on any of the Fridays of Lent devoutly recite after Communion the prayer *En ego, O bone et dulcissime Iesu* before a crucifix.

---

8   *§1, 1°*: EI 1986, conc. 42.
    §1, 2°: EI 1986, conc. 22.

§2   A *partial indulgence* is granted to the faithful who, using any duly approved pious formula, make
  1°   an act of spiritual communion;
  2°   an act of thanksgiving after Communion (e.g., *Anima Christi*; *En ego, O bone et dulcissime Iesu*).

Anima Christi

Soul of Christ, sanctify me.
Body of Christ, save me.
Blood of Christ, inebriate me.
Water from the side of Christ, wash me.
Passion of Christ, strengthen me.
O good Jesus, hear me.
Within thy wounds hide me.
Suffer me not to be separated from thee.
From the malicious enemy defend me.
In the hour of my death call me.
And bid me come to thee,
That with thy saints I may praise thee
for ever and ever.
Amen.

(Roman Missal, Thanksgiving after Mass)

En ego, O bone et dulcissime Iesu

Behold, O kind and most sweet Jesus, I cast myself upon my knees in thy sight, and with the

---

8   §2, *1°*: EI 1986, conc. 15.
     §2, *2°*: EI 1986, conc. 10, 22.

most fervent desire of my soul, I pray and beseech thee that thou wouldst impress upon my heart lively sentiments of faith, hope, and charity, with true contrition for my sins and a firm purpose of amendment; while with deep affection and grief of soul I ponder within myself and mentally contemplate thy five wounds, having before my eyes the words which David the prophet put on thy lips concerning thee: "My hands and my feet they have pierced, they have numbered all my bones."

(*Roman Missal*, Thanksgiving after Mass)

9

EXAMINATION OF CONSCIENCE AND ACT OF CONTRITION

A *partial indulgence* is granted to the faithful who, especially in preparation for sacramental confession,

1° examine their conscience with the purpose of amendment;

2° devoutly recite an act of contrition, according to any legitimate formula (e.g., the *Confiteor*, the psalm *De profundis*, or the psalm *Miserere*, or any of the *gradual* or *penitential psalms*).

---

9   2°: EI 1986, conc. 2, 19, 33.

10

SPIRITUAL EXERCISES AND
MONTHLY RECOLLECTIONS

§1   A *plenary indulgence* is granted to the faithful who
spend at least three entire days in the spiritual exercises
of a retreat.

§2   A *partial indulgence* is granted to the faithful who take
part in a month of recollection.

11

WEEK OF PRAYER FOR CHRISTIAN UNITY

The Catholic Church takes especially to heart the prayer her
Founder offered to the Father the day before he suffered, "That
all may be one!", and therefore she strenuously encourages the
faithful to pray without ceasing for the unity of Christians.

§1   A *plenary indulgence* is granted to the faithful who participate in some of the services during the Week of Christian Unity and assist at the closing of this same week.

§2   A *partial indulgence* is granted to the faithful who
devoutly recite an appropriately approved prayer for the
unity of Christians (e.g. *Omnipotens et misericors Deus*).

Omnipotens et misericors Deus

Almighty and merciful God, who wished to gather
the scattered nations into one people through
your Son, grant that those who glory in the name

---

10   *§1:* EI 1986, conc. 25
      §2: EI 1986, conc. 45.
11   *§2:* EI 1986, conc. 44.

of Christians may put aside division and become one in truth and charity, and that all men may be illumined by the true faith and brought together into the fraternal communion of one Church. Through Christ our Lord. Amen.

12

AT THE POINT OF DEATH

§1 A priest who administers the sacraments to someone in danger of death should not fail to impart the apostolic blessing to which a *plenary indulgence* is attached.

§2 If a priest is unavailable, Holy Mother Church benevolently grants to the Christian faithful, who are duly disposed, a *plenary indulgence* to be acquired at the point of death, provided they have been in the habit of reciting some prayers during their lifetime; in such a case, the Church supplies for the three conditions ordinarily required for a plenary indulgence.

§3 In this latter case, the use of a crucifix or a cross in obtaining the plenary indulgence is commendable.

§4 The faithful can obtain this plenary indulgence at the hour of death, even if they have already acquired a plenary indulgence on that same day.

---

12   §§1-4: EI 1986, conc. 28. (Cf. ID, norms 6, 18; EI 1968, norm 24 §2; *Ordo unctionis infirmorum eorumque pastoralis curae*, December 7, 1972, no. 122; CIC 1983, can. 530; EI 1986, norm 21 §2).

§5   The catechetical instruction of the faithful should ensure that they are duly made aware and frequently reminded of this salutary benefaction of the Church.

13

IN MEMORY OF THE PASSION AND DEATH OF THE LORD

A *plenary indulgence* is granted to the faithful who

§1   devoutly assist at the adoration of the Cross in the solemn liturgical action of Good Friday; or

§2   personally make the pious Way of the Cross, or devoutly unite themselves to the Way of the Cross while it is being led by the Supreme Pontiff and broadcast live on television or radio.

In the pious exercise of the Way of the Cross, we recall anew the sufferings which our divine Redeemer endured while going from the praetorium of Pilate, where he was condemned to death, to Mount Calvary, where he died on the cross for our salvation.

Regarding the acquisition of the plenary indulgence, the following is prescribed:

1.   The pious exercise must be made before stations of the Way of the Cross legitimately erected.

2.   To erect the Way of the Cross, fourteen crosses are needed, to which it is customary to attach a picture or image representing the fourteen stations of Jerusalem.

---

13   *§1:* EI 1986, conc. 17.
      §2: EI 1986, conc. 63.

3. According to common custom, the pious exercise consists of fourteen devotional readings, to which some vocal prayers are added. To make the Way of the Cross, however, it is sufficient to meditate devoutly on the Lord's Passion and Death, and therefore reflection on the particular mysteries of the individual stations is not necessary.

4. Progression from one station to the next is required. If the pious exercise is made publicly, and moving from station to station by all participants is not possible without inconvenience, it is sufficient that at least the one conducting the Way of the Cross progress from station to station, while the others remain in their place.

5. Those legitimately impeded can acquire the same indulgence, if they spend some time, e.g., at least a quarter of an hour, in reading and meditating on the Passion and Death of Our Lord Jesus Christ.

6. Equivalent to the pious exercise of the Way of the Cross, even with regard to obtaining the indulgence, are other pious exercises, approved by competent authority, which call to mind the memory of the Passion and Death of our Lord, likewise with the prescribed fourteen stations.

7. For those belonging to the Eastern Churches, where this pious exercise may not exist, the indulgence can be acquired by means of some other pious exercise in memory of the Passion and Death of our Lord Jesus Christ, accordingly as each patriarch has established for his own faithful.

14

USE OF ARTICLES OF DEVOTION

§1 A *plenary indulgence* is granted to the faithful who, on the Solemnity of the Holy Apostles Peter and Paul, make prayerful use of an article of devotion, as defined by Norm 15, that has been blessed by the Supreme Pontiff or by any bishop, provided the faithful also make a Profession of Faith using any legitimate formula.

§2 A *partial indulgence* is granted to the faithful who devoutly use such articles of devotion properly blessed by either a priest or a deacon.

15

MENTAL PRAYER

A *partial indulgence* is granted to the faithful who for their personal edification devoutly spend time in mental prayer.

16

LISTENING TO SACRED PREACHING

§1 A *plenary indulgence* is granted to the faithful who on the occasion of a mission have heard some of the sermons and are present for the solemn conclusion of the mission.

---

14 EI 1986, conc. 35. To bless articles of devotion properly, the priest or deacon should observe the liturgical formulas of his own Ritual. In special circumstances, he can use the following short form: "In the name of the Father and of the Son + and of the Holy Spirit. Amen" (De Ben., nos. 1165, 1182).

15 EI 1986, conc. 38.

16 EI 1986, conc. 41.

§2 A *partial indulgence* is granted to the faithful who assist with attention and devotion at other occasions of the preaching of the Word of God.

17

PRAYERS TO THE BLESSED VIRGIN MARY

§1 A *plenary indulgence* is granted to the faithful who
  1° devoutly recite the Marian rosary in a church or oratory, or in a family, a religious community, or an association of the faithful, and in general when several of the faithful gather for some honest purpose;
  2° devoutly join in the recitation of the rosary while it is being recited by the Supreme Pontiff and broadcast live by radio or television.
In other circumstances, the indulgence will be *partial*.

The rosary is a prayer formula consisting of fifteen decades of Hail Marys preceded by the Our Father, during the recitation of which we piously meditate on the corresponding mysteries of our redemption.

Regarding the plenary indulgence for the recitation of the Marian rosary, the following is prescribed:

1. The recitation of a third part of the rosary is sufficient, but the five decades must be recited without interruption.
2. Devout meditation on the mysteries is to be added to the vocal prayer.
3. In its public recitation the mysteries must be announced in accord with approved local

17 *§1, 1°*: EI 1986, conc. 48; cf. Pope John Paul II, Apostolic Letter *Rosarium Virginis Mariae* (*On the Most Holy Rosary*) (AAS 95 [2003] 5-36); for the hymn *Akathistos* and the office Paraclisis, cf. conc. 23 below.

custom, but in its private recitation it is sufficient for the faithful simply to join meditation
on the mysteries to the vocal prayer.

§2 A *partial indulgence* is granted to the faithful who
1° devoutly recite the canticle of the *Magnificat*;
2° either at dawn, noon, or evening devoutly recite the
Angelus with its accompanying versicles and prayer
or, during the Easter season, the *Regina caeli*
antiphon with its usual prayer;
3° devoutly address the Blessed Virgin Mary with
some approved prayer (e.g., *Maria, Mater gratiae*;
the *Memorare*; the *Salve Regina*; the *Sancta Maria,
succurre miseris*; or the *Sub tuum praesidium.*)

Angelus Domini

V. The Angel of the Lord declared unto Mary,
R̸. And she conceived of the Holy Spirit.

Hail Mary . . .

V. Behold the handmaid of the Lord,
R̸. Be it done unto me according to thy word.

Hail Mary . . .

V. And the Word was made flesh,
R̸. And dwelt among us.

---

17 §2, 1°: EI 1986, conc. 30.
§2, 2°: EI 1986, conc. 9.
§2, 3°: EI 1986, conc. 31, 32, 51, 52, 57 (cf. conc. 22 below for novenas, litanies, and Little Offices in honor of the Blessed Virgin Mary).

Hail Mary . . .

V. Pray for us, O Holy Mother of God,
R⁄. That we may be made worthy of the promises of Christ.

Let us pray. Pour forth, we beseech thee, O Lord, thy grace into our hearts: that we, to whom the Incarnation of Christ thy Son was made known by the message of an Angel, may by his Passion and Cross be brought to the glory of his Resurrection. Through the same Christ our Lord. Amen.

(*Roman Missal*, Collect for the Fourth Sunday of Advent)

Regina caeli

Queen of Heaven, rejoice, alleluia:
For the Son thou wast privileged to bear, alleluia,
Is risen as he said, alleluia.
Pray for us to God, alleluia.

V. Rejoice and be glad, O Virgin Mary, Alleluia!
R⁄. For the Lord is truly risen, Alleluia.

(*Liturgy of the Hours*, Night Prayer for the Season of Easter)

Let us pray: O God, who gave joy to the world through the Resurrection of thy Son our Lord Jesus Christ, grant, we beseech thee, that through the intercession of the Virgin Mary, his Mother, we may obtain the joys of everlasting life. Through the same Christ our Lord. Amen.

(*Roman Missal*, Collect from the Common of the B.V.M. during the Easter Season)

Maria, Mater gratiae

Mary, Mother of grace and Mother of mercy, shield me from the enemy and receive me at the hour of my death.

Memorare, O piissima Virgo Maria

Remember, O most gracious Virgin Mary, that never was it known that anyone who fled to thy protection, implored thy help, or sought thine intercession was left unaided. Inspired by this confidence, I fly unto thee, O Virgin of virgins, my mother; to thee do I come, before thee I stand, sinful and sorrowful. O Mother of the Word Incarnate, despise not my petitions, but in thy mercy hear and answer me. Amen.

(*Liturgy of the Hours*, Ordinary for Night Prayer)

Salve, Regina

Hail, holy Queen, Mother of mercy; Hail, our life, our sweetness and our hope. To thee do we cry, poor banished children of Eve. To thee do we send up our sighs, mourning and weeping in this valley of tears. Turn then, most gracious advocate, thine eyes of mercy toward us; and after this our exile show unto us the blessed fruit of thy womb, Jesus. O clement, O loving, O sweet Virgin Mary.

(*Liturgy of the Hours*, Night Prayer)

Sancta Maria, succurre miseris

Holy Mary, succor the miserable, help the faint-hearted, comfort the sorrowful, pray for thy people, plead for the clergy, intercede for all women consecrated to God; may all who keep thy holy commemoration feel now thy help and protection.

Sub tuum praesidium

We fly to your patronage, O holy Mother of God; despise not our petitions in our necessities, but deliver us always from all dangers, O glorious and blessed Virgin.

(*Liturgy of the Hours*, Night Prayer)

18

PRAYERS TO ONE'S GUARDIAN ANGEL

A *partial indulgence* is granted to the faithful who devoutly invoke the care of their guardian Angel with a duly approved prayer (e.g. *Angele Dei*).

Angele Dei

Angel of God, my guardian dear, to whom his love entrusts me here, enlighten and guard, rule and guide me. Amen.

---

18   EI 1986, conc. 8.

19

PRAYERS IN HONOR OF ST. JOSEPH

A *partial indulgence* is granted to the faithful who invoke St. Joseph, spouse of the Blessed Virgin Mary, with a duly approved prayer (e.g., *Ad te, beate Ioseph*).

Ad te, beate Ioseph

To you, O blessed Joseph, do we come in our tribulation, and having implored the help of your most holy spouse, we confidently invoke your patronage also. Through that charity which bound you to the Immaculate Virgin Mother of God and through the paternal love with which you embraced the Child Jesus, we humbly beg you graciously to regard the inheritance which Jesus Christ has purchased by his Blood, and with your power and strength to aid us in our necessities. O most watchful Guardian of the Holy Family, defend the chosen children of Jesus Christ; O most loving father, ward off from us every contagion of error and corrupting influence; O our most mighty protector, be kind to us and from heaven assist us in our struggle with the power of darkness. As once you rescued the Child Jesus from deadly peril, so now protect God's Holy Church from the snares of the enemy and from all adversity; shield, too, each one of us by your constant protection, so that, supported by

---

19   EI 1986, conc. 6 (cf. conc. 22, 2°-3° below for litanies and the Little Office of St. Joseph).

your example and your aid, we may be able to live piously, to die in holiness, and to obtain eternal happiness in heaven. Amen.

20

PRAYERS IN HONOR OF THE APOSTLES PETER AND PAUL

A *partial indulgence* is granted to the faithful who devoutly recite the prayer *Sancti Apostoli Petre et Paule.*

Sancti Apostoli Petre et Paule

Holy Apostles Peter and Paul, intercede for us.

Guard your people, who rely on the patronage of your apostles Peter and Paul, O Lord, and keep them under your continual protection. Through Christ our Lord. Amen.

21

PRAYERS IN HONOR OF THE SAINTS AND BLESSEDS

§1 A *partial indulgence* is granted to the faithful who on the memorial of any saint listed in the calendar recite in that saint's honor the prayer taken from the Missal or another one approved by legitimate authority.

---

20   EI 1986, conc. 53.
21   *§1:* EI 1986. conc. 54 (cf. conc. 22, 2° below for litanies of the saints).

§2 In addition, in order to promote the veneration of newly proclaimed saints and blesseds, a *plenary indulgence* is granted a single time within the year following the canonization or beatification to those faithful who make a visit to a church or an oratory in which a solemn celebrations is held in honor of the saint or blessed, and who there devoutly recite the Our Father and the Creed. To any of the faithful who make the aforesaid pious visit during the same period, a *partial indulgence* is granted.

22

NOVENAS, LITANIES, AND THE LITTLE OFFICES

A *partial indulgence* is granted to the faithful who
1° devoutly assist at public novenas (e.g., prior to the Solemnities of the Nativity of the Lord, or of Pentecost, or of the Immaculate Conception of the Blessed Virgin Mary);
2° devoutly recite approved litanies (e.g., of the *Most Holy Name of Jesus*, the *Most Sacred Heart of Jesus*, the *Most Precious Blood of Our Lord Jesus Christ*, the *Blessed Virgin Mary*, *St. Joseph*, and of the *Saints*);
3° piously recite an approved little office (e.g., of the *Passion of Our Lord Jesus Christ*, the *Most Sacred Heart of Jesus*, the *Blessed Virgin Mary*, the *Immaculate Conception*, or *St. Joseph*).

21 *§2*: SPA, decr. September 12, 1968. Cf. SCR, Instr. *De celebrationibus quae in honorem alicuius Sancti vel Beati intra annum a Canonizatione vel Beatificatione peragi solent* (AAS 60 [1968] 602, ad 5).
22 *1°*: EI 1986, conc. 34.
2°: EI 1986, conc. 29.
3°: EI 1986, conc. 36.

Litany of the Holy Name of Jesus

Lord, have mercy	*Lord, have mercy*
Christ, have mercy	*Christ, have mercy*
Lord, have mercy	*Lord, have mercy*
God our Father in heaven	*have mercy on us*
God the Son,	
Redeemer of the world	*have mercy on us*
God the Holy Spirit	*have mercy on us*
Holy Trinity, one God	*have mercy on us*
Jesus, Son of the living God	*have mercy on us*
Jesus, splendor of	
the Father	*have mercy on us*
Jesus, brightness of	
everlasting light	*have mercy on us*
Jesus, king of glory	*have mercy on us*
Jesus, dawn of justice	*have mercy on us*
Jesus, Son of the	
Virgin Mary	*have mercy on us*
Jesus, worthy of our love	*have mercy on us*
Jesus, worthy of	
our wonder	*have mercy on us*
Jesus, mighty God	*have mercy on us*
Jesus, father of the	
world to come	*have mercy on us*
Jesus, prince of peace	*have mercy on us*
Jesus, all-powerful	*have mercy on us*
Jesus, pattern of patience	*have mercy on us*
Jesus, model of obedience	*have mercy on us*

Jesus, gentle and humble of heart	*have mercy on us*
Jesus, lover of chastity	*have mercy on us*
Jesus, lover of us all	*have mercy on us*
Jesus, God of peace	*have mercy on us*
Jesus, author of life	*have mercy on us*
Jesus, model of goodness	*have mercy on us*
Jesus, seeker of souls	*have mercy on us*
Jesus, our God	*have mercy on us*
Jesus, our refuge	*have mercy on us*
Jesus, father of the poor	*have mercy on us*
Jesus, treasure of the faithful	*have mercy on us*
Jesus, Good Shepherd	*have mercy on us*
Jesus, the true light	*have mercy on us*
Jesus, eternal wisdom	*have mercy on us*
Jesus, infinite goodness	*have mercy on us*
Jesus, our way and our life	*have mercy on us*
Jesus, joy of angels	*have mercy on us*
Jesus, king of patriarchs	*have mercy on us*
Jesus, teacher of apostles	*have mercy on us*
Jesus, master of evangelists	*have mercy on us*
Jesus, courage of martyrs	*have mercy on us*
Jesus, light of confessors	*have mercy on us*
Jesus, purity of virgins	*have mercy on us*
Jesus, crown of all saints	*have mercy on us*

Lord, be merciful	*Jesus, save your people*
From all evil	*Jesus, save your people*
From every sin	*Jesus, save your people*

From the snares of the devil	*Jesus, save your people*
From your anger	*Jesus, save your people*
From the spirit of infidelity	*Jesus, save your people*
From everlasting death	*Jesus, save your people*
From neglect of your Holy Spirit	*Jesus, save your people*
By the mystery of your incarnation	*Jesus, save your people*
By your birth	*Jesus, save your people*
By your childhood	*Jesus, save your people*
By your hidden life	*Jesus, save your people*
By your public ministry	*Jesus, save your people*
By your agony and crucifixion	*Jesus, save your people*
By your abandonment	*Jesus, save your people*
By your grief and sorrow	*Jesus, save your people*
By your death and burial	*Jesus, save your people*
By your rising to new life	*Jesus, save your people*
By your return in glory to the Father	*Jesus, save your people*
By your gift of the holy Eucharist	*Jesus, save your people*
By your joy and glory	*Jesus, save your people*

Christ, hear us   *Christ, hear us*
Lord Jesus,
   hear our prayer   *Lord Jesus, hear our prayer*

Lamb of God, you take away
   the sins of the world   *have mercy on us*
Lamb of God, you take away
   the sins of the world   *have mercy on us*
Lamb of God, you take away
   the sins of the world   *have mercy on us*

Let us pray.
Lord, may we who honor the holy name of Jesus enjoy his friendship in this life and be filled with eternal joy in the kingdom where he lives and reigns for ever and ever. Amen.

Litany of the Sacred Heart of Jesus

Lord, have mercy   *Lord, have mercy*
Christ, have mercy   *Christ, have mercy*
Lord, have mercy   *Lord, have mercy*

God our Father in heaven   *have mercy on us*
God the Son,
   Redeemer of the world   *have mercy on us*
God the Holy Spirit   *have mercy on us*
Holy Trinity, one God   *have mercy on us*

Heart of Jesus, Son of the
eternal Father   *have mercy on us*
Heart of Jesus, formed by the
Holy Spirit in the womb of
the Virgin Mother   *have mercy on us*
Heart of Jesus, one with
the eternal Word   *have mercy on us*
Heart of Jesus,
infinite in majesty   *have mercy on us*
Heart of Jesus,
holy temple of God   *have mercy on us*
Heart of Jesus, tabernacle of
the Most High   *have mercy on us*
Heart of Jesus, house of
God and gate of heaven   *have mercy on us*
Heart of Jesus,
aflame with love for us   *have mercy on us*
Heart of Jesus,
source of justice and love   *have mercy on us*
Heart of Jesus,
full of goodness and love   *have mercy on us*
Heart of Jesus,
wellspring of all virtue   *have mercy on us*
Heart of Jesus,
worthy of all praise   *have mercy on us*
Heart of Jesus, king and
center of all hearts   *have mercy on us*
Heart of Jesus,
treasurehouse of
wisdom and knowledge   *have mercy on us*

Heart of Jesus,
  in whom there dwells
  the fullness of God   *have mercy on us*
Heart of Jesus,
  in whom the Father is
  well pleased   *have mercy on us*
Heart of Jesus,
  from whose fullness
  we have all received   *have mercy on us*
Heart of Jesus,
  desire of the eternal hills   *have mercy on us*
Heart of Jesus,
  patient and full of mercy   *have mercy on us*
Heart of Jesus, generous to
  all who turn to you   *have mercy on us*
Heart of Jesus, fountain of
  life and holiness   *have mercy on us*
Heart of Jesus,
  atonement for our sins   *have mercy on us*
Heart of Jesus,
  overwhelmed with insults   *have mercy on us*
Heart of Jesus,
  broken for our sins   *have mercy on us*
Heart of Jesus,
  obedient even to death   *have mercy on us*
Heart of Jesus,
  pierced by a lance   *have mercy on us*
Heart of Jesus,
  source of all consolation   *have mercy on us*

Heart of Jesus,
     our life and resurrection   *have mercy on us*
Heart of Jesus, our peace
     and reconciliation   *have mercy on us*
Heart of Jesus,
     victim of our sins   *have mercy on us*
Heart of Jesus, salvation of
     all who trust in you   *have mercy on us*
Heart of Jesus, hope of
     all who die in you   *have mercy on us*
Heart of Jesus, delight of
     all the saints   *have mercy on us*

Lamb of God, you take away
     the sins of the world   *have mercy on us*
Lamb of God, you take away
     the sins of the world   *have mercy on us*
Lamb of God, you take away
     the sins of the world   *have mercy on us*

Jesus, gentle and humble of heart.
*Touch our hearts and make
them like your own.*

Let us pray.
Father, we rejoice in the gifts of love we have received from the heart of Jesus your Son. Open our hearts to share his life and continue to bless us with his love. We ask this in the name of Jesus the Lord. Amen.

Litany of the Most Precious Blood

Lord, have mercy	*Lord, have mercy*
Christ, have mercy	*Christ, have mercy*
Lord, have mercy	*Lord, have mercy*

God our Father in heaven	*have mercy on us*
God the Son,	
Redeemer of the world	*have mercy on us*
God the Holy Spirit	*have mercy on us*
Holy Trinity, one God	*have mercy on us*

Blood of Christ,	
only Son of the Father	*save us*
Blood of Christ,	
incarnate Word	*save us*
Blood of Christ,	
of the new and eternal covenant	*save us*
Blood of Christ,	
that spilled to the ground	*save us*
Blood of Christ,	
that flowed at the scourging	*save us*
Blood of Christ,	
dripping from the thorns	*save us*
Blood of Christ,	
shed on the cross	*save us*
Blood of Christ,	
the price of our redemption	*save us*
Blood of Christ,	
our only claim to pardon	*save us*
Blood of Christ,	
our blessing cup	*save us*

Blood of Christ,
    in which we are washed   *save us*
Blood of Christ,
    torrent of mercy   *save us*
Blood of Christ,
    that overcomes evil   *save us*
Blood of Christ,
    strength of the martyrs   *save us*
Blood of Christ,
    endurance of the saints   *save us*
Blood of Christ,
    that makes the barren fruitful   *save us*
Blood of Christ,
    protection of the threatened   *save us*
Blood of Christ,
    comfort of the weary   *save us*
Blood of Christ,
    solace of the mourner   *save us*
Blood of Christ,
    hope of the repentant   *save us*
Blood of Christ,
    consolation of the dying   *save us*
Blood of Christ,
    our peace and refreshment   *save us*
Blood of Christ,
    our pledge of life   *save us*
Blood of Christ,
    by which we pass to glory   *save us*
Blood of Christ,
    most worthy of honor   *save us*

Lamb of God, you take away
the sins of the world   *have mercy on us*
Lamb of God, you take away
the sins of the world   *have mercy on us*
Lamb of God, you take away
the sins of the world   *have mercy on us*

Lord, you redeemed us by your blood.
*You have made us a kingdom
to serve our God.*

Let us pray.
Father, by the blood of your Son you have set us free and saved us from death. Continue your work of love within us, that by constantly celebrating the mystery of our salvation we may reach the eternal life it promises. We ask this through Christ our Lord. Amen.

Litany of the Blessed Virgin Mary (Litany of Loreto)

Lord, have mercy   *Lord, have mercy*
Christ, have mercy   *Christ, have mercy*
Lord, have mercy   *Lord, have mercy*

God our Father in heaven   *have mercy on us*
God the Son,
Redeemer of the world   *have mercy on us*
God the Holy Spirit   *have mercy on us*
Holy Trinity, one God   *have mercy on us*

Holy Mary	*pray for us*
Holy Mother of God	*pray for us*
Most honored of virgins	*pray for us*
Mother of Christ	*pray for us*
Mother of the Church	*pray for us*
Mother of divine grace	*pray for us*
Mother most pure	*pray for us*
Mother of chaste love	*pray for us*
Mother and virgin	*pray for us*
Sinless Mother	*pray for us*
Dearest of mothers	*pray for us*
Model of motherhood	*pray for us*
Mother of good counsel	*pray for us*
Mother of our Creator	*pray for us*
Mother of our Savior	*pray for us*
Virgin most wise	*pray for us*
Virgin rightly praised	*pray for us*
Virgin rightly renowned	*pray for us*
Virgin most powerful	*pray for us*
Virgin gentle in mercy	*pray for us*
Faithful Virgin	*pray for us*
Mirror of justice	*pray for us*
Throne of wisdom	*pray for us*
Cause of our joy	*pray for us*
Shrine of the Spirit	*pray for us*
Glory of Israel	*pray for us*
Vessel of selfless devotion	*pray for us*
Mystical Rose	*pray for us*
Tower of David	*pray for us*
Tower of ivory	*pray for us*
House of gold	*pray for us*

Ark of the covenant	*pray for us*
Gate of heaven	*pray for us*
Morning Star	*pray for us*
Health of the sick	*pray for us*
Refuge of sinners	*pray for us*
Comfort of the troubled	*pray for us*
Help of Christians	*pray for us*
Queen of angels	*pray for us*
Queen of patriarchs and prophets	*pray for us*
Queen of apostles and martyrs	*pray for us*
Queen of confessors and virgins	*pray for us*
Queen of all saints	*pray for us*
Queen conceived without sin	*pray for us*
Queen assumed into heaven	*pray for us*
Queen of the rosary	*pray for us*
Queen of families	*pray for us*
Queen of peace	*pray for us*

Lamb of God, you take away
   the sins of the world   *have mercy on us*
Lamb of God, you take away
   the sins of the world   *have mercy on us*
Lamb of God, you take away
   the sins of the world   *have mercy on us*

Pray for us, holy Mother of God.
      That we may become worthy of
         the promises of Christ.

Let us pray.

Eternal God, let your people enjoy constant health in mind and body. Through the intercession of the Virgin Mary free us from the sorrows of this life and lead us to happiness in the life to come. Grant this through Christ our Lord. Amen.

Litany of St. Joseph

Lord, have mercy	*Lord, have mercy*
Christ, have mercy	*Christ, have mercy*
Lord, have mercy	*Lord, have mercy*

God our Father in heaven	*have mercy on us*
God the Son, Redeemer of the world	*have mercy on us*
God the Holy Spirit	*have mercy on us*
Holy Trinity, one God	*have mercy on us*

Holy Mary	*pray for us*
Saint Joseph	*pray for us*
Noble son of the House of David	*pray for us*
Light of patriarchs	*pray for us*
Husband of the Mother of God	*pray for us*
Guardian of the Virgin	*pray for us*
Foster father of the Son of God	*pray for us*
Faithful guardian of Christ	*pray for us*
Head of the holy family	*pray for us*
Joseph, chaste and just	*pray for us*
Joseph, prudent and brave	*pray for us*
Joseph, obedient and loyal	*pray for us*
Pattern of patience	*pray for us*

Lover of poverty	*pray for us*
Model of workers	*pray for us*
Example to parents	*pray for us*
Guardian of virgins	*pray for us*
Pillar of family life	*pray for us*
Comfort of the troubled	*pray for us*
Hope of the sick	*pray for us*
Patron of the dying	*pray for us*
Terror of evil spirits	*pray for us*
Protector of the Church	*pray for us*

Lamb of God, you take away
the sins of the world   *have mercy on us*
Lamb of God, you take away
the sins of the world   *have mercy on us*
Lamb of God, you take away
the sins of the world   *have mercy on us*

God made him master of his household.
And put him in charge of all that he owned.

Let us pray.
Almighty God, in your infinite wisdom and love you chose Joseph to be the husband of Mary, the mother of your Son. As we enjoy his protection on earth may we have the help of his prayers in heaven. We ask this through Christ our Lord. Amen.

Litany of the Saints

Lord, have mercy	*Lord, have mercy*
Christ, have mercy	*Christ, have mercy*
Lord, have mercy	*Lord, have mercy*
Holy Mary, Mother of God	*pray for us*
Saint Michael	*pray for us*
Holy angels of God	*pray for us*
Saint John the Baptist	*pray for us*
Saint Joseph	*pray for us*
Saint Peter and Saint Paul	*pray for us*
Saint Andrew	*pray for us*
Saint John	*pray for us*
Saint Mary Magdalene	*pray for us*
Saint Stephen	*pray for us*
Saint Ignatius of Antioch	*pray for us*
Saint Lawrence	*pray for us*
Saint Perpetua and Saint Felicity	*pray for us*
Saint Agnes	*pray for us*
Saint Gregory	*pray for us*
Saint Augustine	*pray for us*
Saint Athanasius	*pray for us*
Saint Basil	*pray for us*
Saint Martin	*pray for us*
Saint Benedict	*pray for us*
Saint Francis and Saint Dominic	*pray for us*
Saint Francis Xavier	*pray for us*
Saint John Vianney	*pray for us*
Saint Catherine	*pray for us*
Saint Teresa of Jesus	*pray for us*
All holy men and women	*pray for us*

Lord, be merciful   *Lord, deliver us, we pray*
From all evil   *Lord, deliver us, we pray*
From every sin   *Lord, deliver us, we pray*
From everlasting death *Lord, deliver us, we pray*
By your
 coming as man *Lord, deliver us, we pray*
By your death and
 rising to new life *Lord, deliver us, we pray*
By your gift of
 the Holy Spirit *Lord, deliver us, we pray*

Be merciful to us sinners
   Lord, we ask you, hear our prayer
Guide and protect your holy Church
   Lord, we ask you, hear our prayer
Keep the pope and all the clergy in
 faithful service to your Church
   Lord, we ask you, hear our prayer
Bring all peoples together in
 trust and peace
   Lord, we ask you, hear our prayer
Strengthen us in your service
   Lord, we ask you, hear our prayer
Jesus, Son of the living God
   Lord, we ask you, hear our prayer

Christ, hear us   *Christ, hear us*
Christ, graciously hear us
   Christ, graciously hear us

Let us pray.

God of our ancestors who set their hearts on
you, of those who fell asleep in peace, and of
those who won the martyrs' violent crown: we
are surrounded by these witnesses as by clouds
of fragrant incense. In this age we would be
counted in this communion of all the saints; keep
us always in their good and blessed company. In
their midst we make every prayer through Christ
who is our Lord for ever and ever. Amen.

23

PRAYERS OF THE EASTERN CHURCHES

The nature of her catholicity ensures that "each individual part
of the Church contributes through its special gifts to the good
of the whole Church, so that the whole and each part increase"
(LG, no. 13) in every spiritual bounty given by God—whence
prayers from various Eastern traditions have spread also
among the faithful of the Latin rite, especially in recent years,
and are employed with considerable spiritual benefit in both
private and public piety.

§1　A *plenary indulgence* is granted to the faithful who
devoutly recite the *Akathistos* hymn or the *Office of the
Paraclisis* in a church or oratory, or in a family, a religious community, or an association of the faithful, and
in general when several of the faithful gather for some
honest purpose. In other circumstances, *the indulgence
will be partial.*

23　§1: EI 1986, conc. 48 ad 4; PA, decr. *Mater Christi*, May 31, 1991 (in PA, tab.
　　n. 36/91/I).

Regarding the plenary indulgence for the recitation of the hymn *Akathistos*, it need not be recited in full, but it suffices that there be an uninterrupted recitation of some suitable part, according to legitimate custom.

Among the faithful of the Eastern Churches, where the practice of these devotions does not exist, other similar exercises in honor of the Blessed Virgin Mary, as established by the patriarchs, enjoy the same indulgences.

§2 A *partial indulgence* is granted to the faithful who, in accordance with particular times and circumstances, devoutly recite one of the following prayers: a *Prayer of Thanksgiving* (from the Armenian tradition); *Evening Prayer, Prayer for the Faithful Departed* (from the Byzantine Tradition); the *Prayer of the Shrine*, the *Prayer "Lakhu Mara"* known as *To You, O Lord*, (from the Chaldean Tradition); a *Prayer for the Offering of Incense, Prayer to Glorify Mary, the Mother of God* (from the Coptic Tradition); *Prayer for the Remission of Sins, Prayer for Following in the Footsteps of Christ* (from the Ethiopian Tradition); *Prayer for the Church, Prayer After the Celebration of the Liturgy* (from the Maronite Tradition), and the *Intercessions for the Faithful Departed from the Liturgy of St. James* (from the Syro-Antiochian Tradition).

PRAYER OF THE ARMENIAN TRADITION

A Prayer of Thanksgiving for the Church

We thank you, Almighty Father, for having prepared the holy Church for us as a haven of rest, a temple of holiness, where your Holy Trinity is glorified. Alleluia.

We thank you, Christ our King, for having given us life through your vivifying Body and your holy Blood; grant us expiation and great mercy. Alleluia.

We thank you, true Spirit, for having renewed the holy Church; preserve her immaculate, by means of faith in the Trinity, now and forever. Alleluia.

We thank you, O Christ our God, for having given us such a Food of goodness for holiness of life. By means of it preserve us holy and immaculate by living in us with your divine care. Lead us to the pastures of your holy will, O Effecter of good; by means of it fortify us against every snare of the calumniator. Make us worthy to listen to your voice alone, to follow only you, true and victorious Shepherd, and to receive from you the place you prepared for us in your heavenly kingdom, O God and Lord Jesus Christ our Savior, who are blessed with the Father and your Holy Spirit, now and always for ever and ever. Amen.

PRAYERS OF THE BYZANTINE TRADITION
Evening Prayer
In the evening, in the morning, and at noon
we praise you, we bless you,
we give you thanks, and we beg you,
Master of the universe,

grant that our hearts not yield to evil words
but free us from all who try to enslave our souls,
because our eyes are turned to you, O Lord,
and we have placed our hope in you.
Do not abandon us, O God!
For every glory, honor, and adoration is
   due to you,
Father, Son, and Holy Spirit,
now and always and for ever and ever. Amen.

Prayer for the Deceased

God of the spirits and of all flesh, who have
destroyed death and annihilated the devil and
given life to your world, may you yourself, O Lord,
grant to the soul of your deceased servant **N.** rest
in a place of light, a verdant place, a place of fresh-
ness, from where suffering, pain, and cries are far
removed. Do You, O good and compassionate
God, forgive every fault committed by him in
word, work, or thought; because there is no man
who lives and does not sin. You alone are without
sin and your justice is justice throughout the ages
and your word is truth.

    Since you, O Christ our God, are the resur-
rection, the life and the repose of your deceased
servant **N.**, we give you glory together with your
un-begotten Father with your most holy, good,
and vivifying Spirit, now and always and for ever
and ever.

PRAYERS OF THE CHALDEAN TRADITION
Prayer of the Sanctuary

Before the tremendous throne of your majesty, at the exalted place of your divinity, the majestic seat of your glory and the sublime throne of your sovereignty, where your servants the Cherubim continuously sing hymns and where your glorifiers the Seraphim sing unceasingly the "Sanctus," we bow down with fear, adore with trembling, give thanks, and glorify you without ceasing, at all times, O Lord of the universe, Father, Son, and Holy Spirit, for all ages.

The Prayer *"Lakhu Mara"* (To You, O Lord)

When the essence of the sweetness of your love, O Lord our God, will make itself felt in us, and when our souls will be enlightened by the knowledge of your truth, then will we be worthy to go forth to meet your beloved Son as he comes from heaven and there render thanks and glorify you unceasingly in your victorious Church, full of help and happiness, because you are the Lord and Creator of everything, through all ages.

For all the help and the incomprehensible graces that you have granted we give you thanks and we glorify you unceasingly in your victorious Church, full of every help and happiness, because you are Lord and Creator of everything, Father, Son, and Holy Spirit, through all ages.

"Lakhu Mara": To you, O Lord of the universe, we proclaim our confession, and we glorify you, Jesus Christ, because you are the resurrection of our bodies and the savior of our souls.

You indeed, Lord, are the resurrection of our bodies and the good savior of our souls and the everlasting keeper of our life, and we are bound to thank you, adore and glorify you at every moment, O Lord of the universe through all ages.

PRAYERS OF THE COPTIC TRADITION
Prayer of Incense

O King of peace, give us your peace and pardon our sins. Dismiss the enemies of the Church and protect her, so that she never fail.

Emmanuel our God is in our midst in the glory of the Father and of the Holy Spirit.

May he bless us and purify our hearts and cure the sicknesses of our soul and body.

We adore you, O Christ, with your good Father and the Holy Spirit, because you have come and have saved us.

Singing the Praises of Mary

You are raised higher than the Cherubim,
you are extolled above the Seraphim,
because you have drawn down your Son,
and have carried him in your arms,
and nursed him with your milk!
If I say that you are heaven,

behold you are worthy of honor
more than the heavens of heaven,
because he who is above the Cherubim
has come and has taken flesh from you
without harming your virginity!
Blessed are you O Mary! Queen,
O immaculate lamb, O Mother of the King!
Your name will be blessed in all times
by the mouths of the faithful, who will
  shout out saying:
Hail Mary! To you a holy "Ave"!
Hail to her who is worthy of honor
more than all the earth!
Hail Mary! A holy "Ave"!
Hail to the Virgin of all sorrows!
Hail Mary! A holy "Ave"!
Hail to the Queen, to her who is the
  daughter of the King!
Hail Mary! A holy "Ave"!
Hail to the new heaven that is now on earth!
Hail Mary! A holy "Ave"!
Hail to her of whose greatness the
  patriarchs were proud!
Hail Mary! A holy "Ave"!
Hail to her whose honor the prophets foretold!
Indeed, we beg you, O Mary, O queen,
intercede for us with Christ the King.
And you, O Lord, through the intercession of the
  Mother of God, Holy Mary,
give us the grace of the forgiveness of our sins.

PRAYERS OF THE ETHIOPIAN TRADITION
Prayers for the Forgiveness of Sins

O golden thurible, who carried the blessed burning coal, taken from the sanctuary, which forgives sins and destroys crimes: it is the Word of the Lord made flesh in you, who offered himself to his Father, incense and an acceptable sacrifice.

We adore you, O Christ, together with your compassionate, heavenly Father, and your Holy vivifying Spirit, because you have come and have saved us.

O Lord our God, as you once destroyed the walls of Jericho by means of the hand of Joshua your servant, son of Nun, so destroy the walls of my sins and of the sins of your people by means of the hands of me your servant.

A Prayer to Be a Disciple of Christ

O Lord of knowledge and Announcer of wisdom, who have revealed to us what was hidden in the depths of darkness, Giver of the voice of joy to those who preach the breadth of your strength, it is you who in the greatness of your goodness called Paul who first had been a persecutor, and made him into a vessel of election, and you took delight in him, so that he would be an apostle and preacher of the Gospel of your Kingdom. O Christ, our God, you are the lover of men. O kind Lord, give us understanding without weariness, a pure conscience which does not depart from you, so that we know and understand and fully comprehend the measure of your holy doctrine which now comes from him, and as he was the imitator of your life, O Lord, so grant that we be his imitators in works and faith and praise your holy Name and that we glory at all times of the shame of your cross, since yours is the kingdom, the power, the greatness and the might, honor and glory for ever and ever.

PRAYERS OF THE MARONITE TRADITION
A Prayer for the Church

Glory to your mercies, O Christ our King,
Son of God, adored by the universe.
You are our Lord and our God,
the guide of our life and our blessed hope.
You founded on earth a holy Church,
in the image of the one above;
According to this image you formed it;
with love you made her your spouse;
in your mercy you have exalted her;
through your suffering you brought her
    to perfection.
May her loving beauty not be obscured;
may her great richness not be impoverished.
Remember the promise made to Peter
and fulfill your words in reality.
Fortify her gates, secure her locks,
exalt her dignity, raise her ramparts;

bless her children, protect her faithful;
confirm her priests and overcome all those who
   hate her.

A Prayer of Farewell After the Liturgy, Before Leaving the Church

Remain in peace, O Altar of God. May the offering that I have taken from you be for the remission of my debts and the pardon of my sins, and may it obtain for me that I may stand before the tribunal of Christ without damnation and without confusion. I do not know if I will have the opportunity to return and offer another sacrifice upon you. Protect me, O Lord, and preserve your holy Church as the way to truth and salvation. Amen.

PRAYER OF THE SYRO-ANTIOCHIAN TRADITION
Intercession for the Deceased from Liturgy of St. James

Lord, O Lord, God of the pure spirits and of every flesh, be mindful of us all, of those we have remembered and of all we have not remembered and who have left this world with glorious faith. Give repose to their souls, to their bodies, to their spirits. Save them from future damnation and make them worthy of the joy, which is in the bosom of Abraham, Isaac, and Jacob, where the light of your countenance shines, where pain, anguish, and cries are banished. Do not impute to them any fault; do not enter into judgment with your servants, because no living being is justified in your sight and because no man on earth is immune from sin and pure of every filth except for our Lord Jesus Christ, your Son, through whom we, too, hope to obtain mercy and the pardon of our sins and of those of our deceased.

Give rest to their souls; cancel our faults and their faults committed before you willingly or unwillingly, consciously or unconsciously.

Grant them rest. Forgive, O God, and pardon the voluntary and involuntary sins committed consciously or unconsciously by word, work or omissions, by secret thoughts, or publicly, deliberately or through error and which your holy Name knows.

Grant us a Christian ending without sin and unite us at the feet of your elect when you will, where you will and how you will, without us having to blush for our sins because in this as in all things your holy and blessed Name, the Name of our Lord Jesus Christ and of the Holy Spirit, be praised and glorified now and for all ages. Amen.

24

PRAYERS FOR BENEFACTORS

A *partial indulgence* is granted to the faithful who, moved by supernatural gratitude, devoutly recite a duly approved prayer for benefactors (e.g., *Retribuere dignare, Domine*).

---

24   EI 1986, conc. 47.

Retribuere dignare, Domine

May it please you, O Lord, to reward with eternal life all those who do good to us for your Name's sake. Amen.

25

PRAYERS FOR PASTORS

A *partial indulgence* is granted to the faithful who
1° in a spirit of filial devotion, devoutly recite any duly approved prayer for the Supreme Pontiff (e.g., the *Oremus pro Pontifice*);
2° similarly, devoutly recite a prayer taken from the Missal for the bishop of an eparchy or diocese on the occasion of the beginning of his pastoral ministry or on its anniversary.

Oremus pro Pontifice

V. Let us pray for our Sovereign Pontiff N.
R︙. The Lord preserve him and give him life, and make him blessed upon the earth, and deliver him not to the will of his enemies.

26

PRAYERS OF SUPPLICATION AND ACTS OF THANKSGIVING

§1 A *plenary indulgence* is granted to the faithful who devoutly assist either at the recitation or solemn singing of

---

25   *1°*: EI 1986, conc. 39.

1° the *Veni Creator*, either on the first day of the year to implore divine assistance for the course of the whole year, or on the solemnity of Pentecost;

2° the *Te Deum*, on the final day of the year, to offer thanks to God for gifts received throughout the course of the entire year.

§2 A *partial indulgence* is granted to the faithful who,
1° at the beginning and the end of the day,
2° in starting and completing their work,
3° before and after meals,
devoutly offer some legitimately approved prayer of supplication and act of thanksgiving (e.g., *Actiones nostras*; *Adsumus*; *Agimus Tibi gratias*; *Benedic, Domine*; *Domine, Deus Omnipotens*; *Exaudi nos*; the *Te Deum*; the *Veni Creator*; the *Veni Sancte Spiritus*; *Visita, quaesumus, Domine*).

Actiones nostras

Direct, we beseech thee, O Lord, all our actions by thy holy inspiration, carry them on by thy gracious assistance, that every word and work of ours may always begin from thee and by thee be happily ended. Amen.

(A prayer for imploring divine assistance before any work)

(*Roman Missal*, Thursday after Ash Wednesday, Collect; *Liturgy of the Hours*, Monday of the 1st week, Morning Prayer)

---

26 *§1, 1°*: EI 1986, conc. 61.
§1, 2°: EI 1986, conc. 60.
§2: EI 1986, conc. 1, 5, 7, 21, 24, 60, 61, 62, 64.

Adsumus

We have come, O Lord, Holy Spirit, we have come before you, hampered indeed by our many and grievous sins, but for a special purpose gathered together in your name.

Come to us, be with us, and enter our hearts.

Teach us what we are to do and what ought to concern us; show us what we must accomplish, in order that, with your help, we may be able to please you in all things.

May you alone be the author and the finisher of our judgments, who alone with God the Father and his Son possess a glorious name.

Do not allow us to disturb the order of justice, you who love equity above all things. Let not ignorance draw us into devious paths. Let not partiality sway our minds or respect of riches or persons pervert our judgment.

But unite our hearts to you by the gift of your grace alone, that we may be one in you and never forsake the truth; as we are gathered together in your name, so may we in all things hold fast to justice tempered by mercy, that in this life our judgment may never be at variance with you and in the life to come we may attain to everlasting rewards for deeds well done. Amen.

(Prayer before a meeting dealing with matters of common interest)

Agimus tibi gratias

We give You thanks, Almighty God, for all your blessings: who live and reign for ever and ever. Amen.

(A prayer of thanksgiving)

Benedic, Domine

Bless us, O Lord, and these your gifts, which we are about to receive from your bounty, through Christ our Lord. Amen.

(*Book of Blessings*, no. 785)

Domine, Deus omnipotens

Lord, God Almighty, you have brought us safely to the beginning of this day. Defend us today by your mighty power, that we may not fall into any sin, but that all our words may so proceed and all our thoughts and actions be so directed, as to be always just in your sight. Through Christ our Lord. Amen.

(*Liturgy of the Hours*, Monday Morning Prayer of Week Two)

Exaudi nos

Hear us, Lord, holy Father, almighty and eternal God; and graciously send your holy angel from heaven to watch over, to cherish, to protect, to abide with, and to defend all who dwell in this house. Through Christ our Lord. Amen.

Veni, Sancte Spiritus

Come, Holy Spirit, fill the hearts of your faithful and enkindle in them the fire of your love.

(*Liturgy of the Hours*, Pentecost Sunday)

Visita, quaesumus, Domine

Visit, we beg you, O Lord, this dwelling, and drive from it all snares of the enemy: let your holy Angels dwell herein, to keep us in peace; and let your blessing be always upon us. Through Christ our Lord. Amen.

(*Liturgy of the Hours*, Night Prayer for Solemnities)

27

A PRIEST'S FIRST MASS AND JUBILEE CELEBRATIONS OF ORDINATION

§1 A *plenary indulgence* is granted to
   1° a priest celebrating his first Mass before the people on a chosen day;
   2° the faithful who devoutly assist at such a Mass.

§2 Similarly, a *plenary indulgence* is granted to
   1° priests celebrating the twenty-fifth, fiftieth, sixtieth, and seventieth anniversary of their priestly ordinations, who renew before God their promise of faithfully fulfilling the duties of their vocation;

---

27 §1: EI 1986, conc. 43.
    §2, 1°: EI 1986, conc. 49.

2° bishops celebrating the twenty-fifth, fortieth, and fiftieth anniversaries of their episcopal ordination, who renew before God their promise of faithfully fulfilling the duties of their office;

3° the faithful who devoutly assist at jubilee Mass celebrations.

28

PROFESSION OF FAITH AND
ACTS OF THE THEOLOGICAL VIRTUES

§1 A *plenary indulgence* is granted to the faithful who, at the celebration of the Easter Vigil or on the anniversary of their own Baptism, renew their baptismal vows in any legitimately approved formula.

§2 A *partial indulgence* is granted to the faithful who
1° renew their baptismal vows in any formula;
2° devoutly sign themselves with the sign of the cross, using the customary words: *In the name of the Father and of the Son and of the Holy Spirit. Amen*;
3° devoutly recite either the Apostles' Creed or the Niceno-Constantinopolitan Creed;
4° recite an Act of Faith, Hope, and Charity in any legitimate formula.

---

27 §2, 3°: EI 1986, conc. 49.
28 §1: EI 1986, conc. 70.
    §2, 1°: EI 1986, conc. 70.
    §2, 2°: EI 1986, conc. 55.
    §2, 3°: EI 1986, conc. 16.
    §2, 4°: EI 1986, conc. 2 (each act is enriched with an indulgence).

29

FOR THE FAITHFUL DEPARTED

§1 A *plenary indulgence*, applicable only to the souls in purgatory, is granted to the faithful who,

1° on any and each day from November 1 to 8, devoutly visit a cemetery and pray, if only mentally, for the departed;

2° on All Souls' Day (or, according to the judgment of the ordinary, on the Sunday preceding or following it, or on the solemnity of All Saints), devoutly visit a church or an oratory and recite an Our Father and the Creed.

§2 A *partial indulgence*, applicable only to the souls in purgatory, is granted to the faithful who

1° devoutly visit a cemetery and at least mentally pray for the dead;

2° devoutly recite lauds or vespers from the Office of the Dead or the prayer *Eternal rest.*

Requiem aeternam

Eternal rest grant unto them, O Lord, and let perpetual light shine upon them. May they rest in peace.

(*Order of Christian Funerals*)

---

29   §1, 1°: EI 1986, conc. 13.
     §1, 2°: EI 1986, conc. 67 (cf. also norm 19, above).
     §2, 1°: EI 1986, conc. 13.
     §2, 2°: EI 1986, conc. 18, 46.

30

READING OF SACRED SCRIPTURE

§1   A *plenary indulgence* is granted to the faithful who read the Sacred Scriptures as spiritual reading, from a text approved by competent authority and with the reverence due to the divine word, for at least a half an hour; if the time is less, the indulgence will be *partial.*

§2   If for some good reason a person is unable to read the Sacred Scriptures, a *plenary* or *partial indulgence* is granted, as above, if the text of Sacred Scripture is listened to while another person is reading or if it is heard by means of a video or audio recording.

31

A DIOCESAN SYNOD

A *plenary indulgence* is granted a single time to the faithful who, during a diocesan synod, devoutly visit the church in which the synod is celebrated and there recite an Our Father and the Creed.

32

A PASTORAL VISIT

A *plenary indulgence* is granted a single time to the faithful who, during the time of a pastoral visit, assist at the sacred functions over which the visitator presides.

---

30   *§1:* EI 1986, conc. 50.
31   EI 1986, conc. 58.
32   EI 1986, conc. 69.

33

VISITING SACRED PLACES

§1   A *plenary indulgence* is granted to the faithful who visit, and there devoutly recite an Our Father and the Creed,

1°   one of the four Patriarchal Basilicas in Rome, either as part of group making a pilgrimage to the basilica, or at least with the purpose of expressing during the visit filial submission to the Roman Pontiff;

2°   a minor basilica

a.   on the solemnity of the holy Apostles Peter and Paul;

b.   on the solemnity of its Titular;

c.   on August 2, the day of the "Portiuncula" indulgence;

d.   once a year, on a day chosen by the Christian faithful;

3°   the cathedral church

a.   on the solemnity of the holy Apostles Peter and Paul,

b.   on the solemnity of its Titular;

c.   on the liturgical celebration of the Cathedral of St. Peter, the Apostle;

d.   on the dedication of the Archbasilica of the Most Holy Savior;

e.   on August 2, the day of the "Portiuncula" indulgence;

---

33   *§1, 1°:* EI 1986, conc. 11.

§1, 2°: Cf SCR, decr. *Domus Dei*, June 6, 1968 (AAS 60 [1968] 536-539). Both indulgences, under letters b and c, can be gained either on the designated day or on another day which the Ordinary will designate for the good of the faithful (also 3°b, e; 4°a; 5°a, b).

§1, 3°: EI 1986, conc. 65.

4° an international, national, or diocesan shrine established by competent authority
  a. on the solemnity of its Titular;
  b. once a year, on a day chosen by the Christian faithful;
  c. as often as they assist in a group pilgrimage visiting the shrine;
5° a parish church
  a. on the solemnity of its Titular;
  b. on August 2, the day of the "Portiuncula" indulgence;
6° a church or an altar on the day of its dedication;
7° a church or an oratory of institutes of consecrated life and societies of apostolic life, on the liturgical memorial of their founder.

§2 Similarly, a *plenary indulgence* is granted to the faithful who assist in the sacred functions held in any stational church on its designated day; if they merely visit the church devoutly, the *indulgence will be partial.*

§3 A *partial indulgence* is granted to the faithful who devoutly visit one of the ancient Christian cemeteries or catacombs.

---

33 §1, 4°: Cf. CIC, cann. 1230-1234.
§1, 5°: EI 1986, conc. 65. The co-cathedral church—if there is one—even if it is not a parish church, and quasi parish churches enjoy the same indulgences: cf. CIC, can. 516 §1. For those sailing and for sailors cf. Pope John Paul II, Motu proprio *Stella Maris* (AAS 89 [1997] 209-216).
§1, 6°: EI 1986, conc. 66.
§1, 7°: EI 1986, conc. 68.
§2: EI 1986, conc. 56. Cf. CE, nos. 260-261.
§3: EI 1986, conc. 14.

Appendices

PIOUS INVOCATIONS

The following points are to be noted in regard to pious invocations:

1. An invocation, in relation to an indulgence, is not to be considered a complete or distinct work in itself, but rather is to be used as a complement to some other work by which the faithful raise their minds to God in humble trust, while carrying out their duties and bearing the hardships of life. Hence, a pious invocation completes the elevation of the mind to God; both the raising up of the mind and the pious invocation are like a precious stone which is inserted into ordinary activities to adorn them, or are like salt which properly seasons these same activities.[1]

2. The invocation to be preferred is the one which is more in harmony with the particular situation and the personal dispositions of the individual: whether it comes spontaneously to mind or is chosen from those proven effective in their long-standing use by the Christian faithful. A short list of these is added below.

3. An invocation can be very short, expressed either in just one or a few words, or even merely conceived in the mind.
   The following are presented by way of example: My God!—Father!—Jesus!—Praised be Jesus Christ! (or another customary Christian greeting)—I believe in you, O Lord!—I

---

1   Cf. Rom 8:15 and Gal 4:6.

adore you!—I hope in you!—I love you!—All for you!—
Thanks be to you!—(*or* Thanks be to God!)—Blessed be God!
(*or* Let us bless the Lord!)—Your kingdom come!—Your will
be done!—As the Lord wills!—Help me, O God!—Comfort
me!—Hear me! (*or* Hear my prayer!)—Save me!—Have mercy
on me!—Spare me, O Lord!—Do not allow me to be separated
from you!—Do not forsake me!—Hail, Mary!—Glory to God
in the highest!—You are great, O Lord![2]—I am totally yours!

EXAMPLES OF INVOCATIONS CURRENTLY IN USE[3]

Allow me to praise you, Virgin most holy; give me
strength against your enemies.

All holy men and women of God, pray for us.

Blessed be the Holy Trinity

Christ conquers! Christ reigns! Christ rules!

Father, into your hands I commend my spirit.[4]

Glory be to the Father and to the Son and to the
Holy Spirit.

Hail, O Cross, our only hope.

Heart of Jesus, all for you.

Heart of Jesus, burning with love for us, inflame
our hearts with love for you.

Heart of Jesus, in you I trust.

Holy Mary, Mother of God, pray for me.

Holy Mother of God, ever Virgin Mary,
intercede for us.

Jesus, gentle and humble of heart, make my heart
like unto yours.

2   Cf. Jud 16:16 and Ps 86 [Vg 85]:10.
3   Others can be found in common prayer books.
4   Lk 23:46; cf. Ps 31 [Vg 30]:6.

Jesus, Mary and Joseph.

Jesus, Mary and Joseph, I give you my heart and
my soul. Jesus, Mary and Joseph, assist me
in my last agony. Jesus, Mary and Joseph,
may I breathe forth my soul in peace with you.

Lord, increase our faith.[5]

Lord, let our minds be united in truth, and our
hearts in love.

Lord, save us, we are perishing.[6]

Lord, send laborers into your harvest.[7]

May the Virgin Mary bless us with her holy child.

May the most Blessed Sacrament be praised
now and forevermore.

Merciful Lord Jesus, grant them rest.

Most Sacred Heart of Jesus, have mercy on us.

Mother of Sorrows, pray for us.

My God and my all.

My Lord and my God![8]

My Mother, my trust.

O God, be merciful to me a sinner.[9]

O Queen conceived without original sin,
pray for us.

Pray for us, O holy Mother of God, that we may
be made worthy of the promises of Christ.

Remain with us, O Lord.[10]

---

5 Lk 17:5.
6 Mt 8:25.
7 Cf. Mt 9:38.
8 Jn 20:28.
9 Lk 18:13.
10 Cf. Lk 24:29.

Teach me to do your will, for you are my God.[11]
Tender heart of Mary, be my safety!
You are the Christ, the Son of the living God.[12]
We adore you, O Christ, and we bless you,
    because by your holy Cross you have
    redeemed the world.

---

11 Ps 143:10.
12 Mt 16:16.

APOSTOLIC PENITENTIARY

DECREE

INDULGENCES ATTACHED TO DEVOTIONS IN HONOR OF DIVINE MERCY

"O God, your mercy knows no bounds and the treasure of your goodness is infinite . . ." (*Prayer after the* "Te Deum" *Hymn*) and "O God, you reveal your almighty power above all by showing mercy and forgiveness . . ." (*Prayer for the Twenty-Sixth Sunday of Ordinary Time*): in these prayers Holy Mother Church humbly and faithfully sings of Divine Mercy. Indeed, God's great patience with the human race in general and with each individual person shines out in a special way when sins and moral failures are forgiven by Almighty God Himself and the guilty are readmitted in a fatherlike way to his friendship, which they deservedly lost.

Duty of honoring Divine Mercy

The faithful with deep spiritual affection are drawn to commemorate the mysteries of divine pardon and to celebrate them devoutly. They clearly understand the supreme benefit, indeed the duty, that the People of God have to praise Divine Mercy with special prayers and, at the same time, they realize that by gratefully performing the works required and satisfying the necessary conditions, they can obtain spiritual benefits that derive from the Treasury of the Church. "The paschal mystery is the culmination of this revealing and effecting of mercy, which is able to justify man, to restore justice in the sense of that salvific order which God willed from the beginning in man, and through man, in the world" (Encyclical Letter *Dives in misericordia*, no. 7).

It is God's Mercy that grants supernatural sorrow and resolution to amend

Indeed, Divine Mercy knows how to pardon even the most serious sins, and in doing so it moves the faithful to perceive a supernatural, not merely psychological, sorrow for their sins so that, ever with the help of divine grace, they may make a firm resolution not to sin any more. Such spiritual dispositions undeniably follow upon the forgiveness of mortal sin when the faithful fruitfully receive the sacrament of Penance or repent of their sin with an act of perfect charity and perfect contrition, with the resolution to receive the sacrament of Penance as soon as they can. Indeed, Our Lord Jesus Christ teaches us in the parable of the Prodigal Son that the sinner must confess his misery to God saying: "Father I have sinned against heaven and against you; I am no longer worthy to be called your son" (Lk 15:18-19), realizing that this is a work of God, "for [he] was dead, and is alive; he was lost, and is found" (Lk 15:32).

Second Sunday of Easter, Divine Mercy Sunday

And so with provident pastoral sensitivity and in order to impress deeply on the souls of the faithful these precepts and teachings of the Christian faith, the Supreme Pontiff, John Paul II, moved by the consideration of the Father of Mercy, has willed that the Second Sunday of Easter be dedicated to recalling with special devotion these gifts of grace and gave this Sunday the name "Divine Mercy Sunday" (Congregation for Divine Worship and the Discipline of the Sacraments, Decree *Misericors et miserator*, May 5, 2000).

The Gospel of the Second Sunday of Easter narrates the wonderful things Christ the Lord accomplished on the day of the Resurrection during his first public appearance: "On the evening of that day, the first day of the week, the doors being shut where the disciples were, for fear of the Jews, Jesus came and stood among them and said to them, 'Peace be with you.' When he said this, he showed them his hands and his side. Then the discples were glad to see the Lord. Jesus said to them again, 'Peace be with you. As the Father has sent me, even so I send you.' And then he breathed on them, and said to them, 'Receive the Holy Spirit. If you forgive the sins of any, they are forgiven; if you retain the sins of any, they are retained'" (Jn 20:19-23).

Plenary Indulgence

To ensure that the faithful would observe this day with intense devotion, the Supreme Pontiff himself established that this Sunday be enriched by a plenary indulgence, as will be explained below, so that the faithful might receive in great abundance the gift of the consolation of the Holy Spirit. In this way, they can foster a growing love for God and for their neighbor, and after they have obtained God's pardon, they in turn might be persuaded to show a prompt pardon to their brothers and sisters.

Pardon of others who sin against us

Thus the faithful will more closely conform to the spirit of the Gospel, receiving in their hearts the renewal that the Second

Vatican Council explained and introduced: "Mindful of the words of the Lord: 'By this all men will know that you are my disciples, if you have love for one another' (Jn 13:35), Christians can yearn for nothing more ardently than to serve the men of this age with an ever growing generosity and success. . . . It is the Father's will that we should recognize Christ our brother in the persons of all men and love them with an effective love, in word and in deed" (Pastoral Constitution, *Gaudium et spes*, no. 93).

Three conditions for the plenary indulgence

And so the Supreme Pontiff, motivated by an ardent desire to foster in Christians this devotion to Divine Mercy as much as possible in the hope of offering great spiritual fruit to the faithful, in the Audience granted on June 13, 2002, to those Responsible for the Apostolic Penitentiary, granted the following Indulgences:

- a *plenary indulgence*, granted under the usual conditions (sacramental confession, Eucharistic communion and prayer for the intentions of Supreme Pontiff) to the faithful who, on the Second Sunday of Easter or Divine Mercy Sunday, in any church or chapel, in a spirit that is completely detached from the affection for a sin, even a venial sin, take part in the prayers and devotions held in honour of Divine Mercy, or who, in the presence of the Blessed Sacrament exposed or reserved in the tabernacle, recite the Our Father and the Creed, adding a devout prayer to the merciful Lord Jesus (e.g., "Merciful Jesus, I trust in you!");

- a *partial indulgence*, granted to the faithful who, at least with a contrite heart, pray to the merciful Lord Jesus a legitimately approved invocation.

For those who cannot go to church or the seriously ill

In addition, sailors working on the vast expanse of the sea; the countless brothers and sisters, whom the disasters of war, political events, local violence and other such causes have been driven out of their homeland; the sick and those who nurse them; and all who for a just cause cannot leave their homes or who carry out an activity for the community which cannot be postponed may obtain a plenary indulgence on Divine Mercy Sunday, if totally detesting any sin, as has been said before, and with the intention of fulfilling as soon as possible the three usual conditions, will recite the Our Father and the Creed before a devout image of Our Merciful Lord Jesus and, in addition, pray a devout invocation to the Merciful Lord Jesus (e.g., "Merciful Jesus, I trust in you").

If it is impossible that people do even this, on the same day they may obtain the *plenary indulgence* if with a spiritual intention they are united with those carrying out the prescribed practice for obtaining the indulgence in the usual way and offer to the Merciful Lord a prayer and the sufferings of their illness and the difficulties of their lives, with the resolution to accomplish as soon as possible the three conditions prescribed to obtain the plenary indulgence.

Duty of priests: Inform parishioners, hear confessions, lead prayers

Priests who exercise pastoral ministry, especially parish priests, should inform the faithful in the most suitable way of the

Church's salutary provision. They should promptly and generously be willing to hear their confessions. On Divine Mercy Sunday, after celebrating Mass or Vespers, or during devotions in honour of Divine Mercy, with the dignity that is in accord with the rite, they should lead the recitation of the prayers that have been given above. Finally, since "Blessed are the merciful, for they shall obtain mercy" (Mt 5:7), when they instruct their people, priests should gently encourage the faithful to practise works of charity or mercy as often as they can, following the example of, and in obeying the commandment of Jesus Christ, as is listed for the second general concession of indulgence in the *Enchiridion indulgentiarum*.

This Decree has perpetual force, any provision to the contrary notwithstanding.

+ Archbishop Luigi De Magistris
Titular Archbishop of Nova
Major Pro-Penitentiary

Fr. Gianfranco Girotti, OFM Conv
Regent

APOSTOLIC PENITENTIARY

DECREE

For the greater spiritual good of the faithful, eparchial and diocesan bishops are granted the faculty of imparting the Papal Blessing with the attendant plenary indulgence once a year, in the co-cathedral churches which were formerly the cathedrals of eparchies or dioceses that no longer exist as dioceses or eparchies. In no way does this grant diminish the triple concession established by law for each particular Church.

The cathedral church, "with the majesty of its architectural structure, represents the spiritual temple that is built within each soul in the splendor of grace, in accordance with the Apostle's words: 'You in fact are the temple of the living God'" (2 Cor 6:16). The cathedral is also a powerful symbol of the visible Church of Christ who prays, sings and worships on this earth; that is, it should be seen as an image of the mystical Body whose members are united through charity and nourished by the outpouring of supernatural gifts (cf. Paul VI, Apostolic Constitution *Mirificus eventus*, no. 72, December 7, 1965).

It is very profitable for the faithful to feel a special bond of affection for the cathedral church, the most noble seat and symbol of the bishop's magisterium and liturgical ministry. Indeed, on the one hand, with this religious disposition the faithful express their recognition and veneration for *the certain charism of truth* (cf. St Irenaeus of Lyons, *Ad haereses*, Book IV, c. 40, no. 2), with which the bishops are endowed who are hierarchically united with the Bishop of Rome, Vicar of Christ; and, on the other hand, they wish to participate in and, insofar as they are empowered, celebrate the sacred realities in communion with the Pastor who on earth represents the *Eternal Shepherd and Bishop of our souls* (cf. 1 Pt 2:25).

In recent times, new social, geographical and economic shifts, new lifestyles, the unfortunate reduction in number of sacred ministers in many regions that had an ancient Catholic tradition, and the justifiable need to coordinate pastoral activity have led to the suppression of some particular Churches, while their territory and population have been merged with that of the bishop of a larger particular Church.

However, out of consideration for their venerable antiquity, for famous historical events or for the remarkable degree of holiness which flourished among many of the faithful of these former particular Churches, to those church buildings that at one time had been cathedrals the title of co-cathedral was given for the precise purpose of fostering the devotion of the faithful to their previous church, while preserving the wholly spiritual and canonical communion with their bishop who is bound by a privileged bond to the present cathedral.

Approving these filial sentiments and desiring to make them ever more spiritually perfect, the Supreme Pontiff John Paul II, at an audience granted on June 13, 2002, to the undersigned Superiors of the Apostolic Penitentiary, established that bishops in those churches that had once been cathedrals, and today are co-cathedrals existing in their territory, without prejudice to the provision that allows for the Papal Blessing to be imparted in the Cathedral on three Solemnities in the year, as established in art. no. 7 §2 of the *Enchiridion Indulgentiarum*, have the faculty to impart the Papal Blessing along with a plenary indulgence once a year, on the celebration of a solemnity that the bishops themselves will designate. In this way the faithful present in these co-cathedral churches can receive the blessing and indulgence, in a spirit that is detached from all affection for any sin, and under the usual conditions required for receiving a plenary indulgence (sacramental confession, Eucharistic communion and prayer according to the Supreme Pontiff's intentions). The present Decree is perpetually valid, notwithstanding anything to the contrary.

Given in Rome, at the offices of the Apostolic Penitentiary, June 29, 2002, on the Solemnity of the Apostles, Sts. Peter and Paul.

+ Archbishop Luigi De Magistris
Titular Archbishop of Nova,
Major Pro-Penitentiary

Rt. Rev. Gianfranco Girotti, OFM Conv.
Regent

TEXT OF THE
APOSTOLIC CONSTITUTION
INDULGENTIARUM DOCTRINA
OF POPE PAUL VI

Apostolic Constitution
Indulgentiarum doctrina

PAUL, BISHOP
SERVANT OF THE SERVANTS OF GOD
AD PERPETUAM REI MEMORIAM

I.

1. The doctrine and practice of indulgences which have been in force for many centuries in the Catholic Church have a solid foundation in divine revelation[1] which comes from the Apostles and "develops in the Church with the help of the Holy Spirit," while "as the centuries succeed one another the Church constantly moves forward toward the fullness of divine truth until the words of God reach their complete fulfillment in her."[2]

For an exact understanding of this doctrine and of its beneficial use it is necessary, however, to remember truths which the entire Church illumined by the Word of God has always believed and which the bishops, the successors of the Apostles, and first and foremost among them the Roman Pontiffs, the successors of Peter, have taught by means of pastoral

---

1   Cf. Council of Trent, Session 25, *Decree on Indulgences* (DS 1835); cf. Mt 28:18.
2   Second Vatican Council, Dogmatic Constitution on Divine Revelation, no. 8 (AAS 58 [1966] 821); cf. First Vatican Council, Dogmatic Constitution on the Catholic Faith, ch. 4 "On Faith and Reason" (DS 3020).

practice as well as doctrinal documents throughout the course of centuries to this day.

2. It is a divinely revealed truth that sins bring punishments inflicted by God's sanctity and justice. These must be expiated either on this earth through the sorrows, miseries and calamities of this life and above all through death,[3] or else in the life beyond through fire and torments or "purifying" punishments.[4] Therefore it has always been the conviction of the faithful that the

---

3   Cf. Gen 3:16-19: "To the woman [God] said: 'I will make great your distress in child-bearing; in pain shall you bring forth children; for your husband shall be your longing, though he have dominion over you.' and to Adam he said: 'Because you have listened to your wife, and have eaten of the tree of which I commanded you not to eat: Cursed be the ground because of you; in toil shall you eat of it all the days of your life; thorns and thistles shall it bring forth to you. . . . In the sweat of your brow you shall eat bread, till you return to the ground, since out of it you were taken; for dust you are and unto dust you shall return.'"
    Cf. also Lk 19:41-44; Rom 2:9; and 1 Cor 11:30.
    Cf. AUGUSTINE, *Exposition on Psalm 58 1:13*—"Every sin, whether small or great, must be punished, either by man himself doing penance, or by God chastising him": CCL 39, p. 739; PL 36, 701.
    Cf. THOMAS, *S. Th.* 1-2, q. 87, a. 1: "And because sin is an inordinate act, it is evident that whoever sins commits an offense against an order; wherefore he is put down, in consequence, by that same order. This repression is punishment."

4   Cf. Mt 25:41-42: "Depart from me, accursed ones, into the everlasting fire which was prepared for the devil and his angels. For I was hungry and you did not give me to eat." Cf. also Mk 9:42-43; Jn 5:28-29; Rom 2:9; Gal 6:6-8.
    Cf. SECOND COUNCIL OF LYONS, Session 4, *Profession of faith of Emperor Michael Palaeologus* (DS 856-858).
    Cf. COUNCIL OF FLORENCE, *Decree for the Greeks* (DS 1304-1306).
    Cf. AUGUSTINE, *Enchiridion*, 66,17: "Many sins, likewise, seem now to be overlooked and visited with no punishments, but the penalties for these are reserved for the time to come; for it is not in vain that that day is called the day of judgment in which the Judge of the living and the dead is to come. On the other hand, sins are punished now and will, provided they are pardoned, inflict no harm in the life to come. Accordingly, concerning certain temporal punishments inflicted on sinners in this life, the Apostle, referring to those whose sins have been blotted out and not reserved for the final judgment, says (1 Cor 11:31-32): 'For if we judged ourselves, we would not be judged by the Lord; but when we are judged, we are being chastised by the Lord, that we may not be condemned with the world'": ed. Scheel, Tubingen 1930, p. 42; PL 40, 263.

paths of evil are fraught with many stumbling blocks and bring adversities, bitterness and harm to those who follow them.[5]

These punishments are imposed by the just and merciful judgment of God for the purification of souls, the defense of the sanctity of the moral order and the restoration of the glory of God to its full majesty. Every sin in fact causes a perturbation in the universal order established by God in His ineffable wisdom and infinite charity, and the destruction of immense values with respect to the sinner himself and to the human community. Christians throughout history have always regarded sin not only as a transgression of divine law but also—though not always in a direct and evident way—as contempt for or disregard of the friendship between God and man,[6] just as they have regarded it as a real and unfathomable offense against God and indeed an ungrateful rejection of the love of God shown us through Jesus Christ, who called His disciples friends and not servants.[7]

3. It is therefore necessary for the full remission and—as it is called—reparation of sins not only that friendship with God be re-established by a sincere conversion of the mind and amends

5   Cf. *The Shepherd of Hermas*, Mand. 6, 1, 3: Funk, *The Apostolic Fathers 1*, 487.
6   Cf. Is 1:2-3: "Sons have I raised and reared, but they have disowned me. An ox knows its owner, and an ass, its master's manger. But Israel does not know, my people has not understood." Cf. also Dt 8:11, 32:15ff.; Ps 105:21 and 118, passim; Wis 7:14; Is 17:10, 44:21; Jer 33:8; Ez 20:27.
    Cf. SECOND VATICAN COUNCIL, Dogmatic Constitution on Divine Revelation *Dei Verbum*, no. 2: "Through this revelation, therefore, the invisible God (see Col 1:15; 1 Tm 1:17) out of the abundance of his charity speaks to men as friends (see Ex 33:11; Jn 15:14-15) and dwells with them (see Bar 3:38) in order that he may invite and receive them into fellowship with himself" (AAS 58 [1966] 818). Cf. also ibid., no. 21: loc. cit., 827-828.
7   Cf. Jn 15:14-15.
    Cf. SECOND VATICAN COUNCIL, Pastoral Constitution on the Church in the Modern World *Gaudium et spes*, no. 22 (AAS 58 [1966] 1042), and the Decree on the Missionary Activity of the Church *Ad gentes divinitus*, no. 13 (AAS 58 [1966] 962).

made for the offense against His wisdom and goodness, but also that all the personal as well as social values and those of the universal order itself, which have been diminished or destroyed by sin, be fully reintegrated whether through voluntary reparation which will involve punishment or through acceptance of the punishments established by the just and most holy wisdom of God, from which the sanctity and the splendor of His glory will shine forth throughout the world. The very existence and the gravity of the punishment enable us to understand the foolishness and malice of sin and its harmful consequences.

That punishment or the vestiges of sin may remain to be expiated or cleansed and that they in fact frequently do even after the remission of guilt[8] is clearly demonstrated by the doc-

---

8   Cf. Num 20:12: "But the Lord said to Moses and Aaron: 'Because you were not faithful to me in showing forth my sanctity before the Israelites, you shall not lead this community into the land I shall give them.'"

    Cf. Num 27:13-14: "When you have viewed it, you too shall be taken to your people, as was your brother Aaron, because in the rebellion of the community in the desert of Sin you both rebelled against my order to manifest my sanctity to them by means of the water."

    Cf. 2 Sam 12:13-14: "And David said to Nathan: 'I have sinned against the Lord.' And Nathan said to David: 'The Lord also has taken away your sin; you shall not die. Nevertheless, because you have given occasion to the enemies of the Lord to blaspheme, for this thing the child, that is born to you, shall surely die.'"

    Cf. INNOCENT IV, *Instruction for the Greeks* (DS 838).

    Cf. COUNCIL OF TRENT, Session 6, can. 30: "If anyone should say that, after having received the grace of justification, the guilt of the repentant sinner and his debt of eternal punishment are so cancelled that no debt of temporal punishment remains, to be satisfied, before he can enter into the kingdom of heaven, either in this life or in the life to come in purgatory: let him be anathema" (DS 1580); cf. also DS 1689, 1693.

    Cf. AUGUSTINE, *Tract on the Gospel of John*, 124, 5: "Man is obliged to suffer (in this life) even when his sins are forgiven, although it was the first sin that caused his falling into this misery. For the penalty is of longer duration than the guilt, lest the guilt should be accounted small, were the penalty also to end with it. It is for this reason—either to make manifest the indebtedness of his misery, or to correct his frailty in this life, or to exercise him in necessary patience—that man is held in this life to the penalty, even when he is no longer held to the guilt unto eternal damnation": CCL 36, pp. 683-684; PL 35, 1972-1973.

trine on purgatory. In purgatory, in fact, the souls of those "who died in the charity of God and truly repentant, but before satisfying with worthy fruits of penance for sins committed and for omissions"[9] are cleansed after death with purgatorial punishments. This is also clearly evidenced in the liturgical prayers with which the Christian community admitted to Holy Communion has addressed God since most ancient times: "that we, who are justly subjected to afflictions because of our sins, may be mercifully set free from them for the glory of thy name."[10]

For all men who walk this earth daily commit at least venial sins;[11] thus all need the mercy of God to be set free from the penal consequences of sin.

---

9   SECOND COUNCIL OF LYONS, Session 4 (DS 856).

10 Cf. *Roman Missal*, Oration for Septuagesima Sunday: "O Lord, in your kindness hear the prayers of your people. We are being justly punished for our sins, but be merciful and free us for the glory of your name."

     Cf. *Roman Missal*, Monday after First Sunday in Lent, Oration over the People: "Free us from the slavery of our sins, O Lord, and mercifully shield us from the punishments these sins deserve."

     Cf. *Roman Missal*, Third Sunday in Lent, Prayer after Communion: "O God, you have allowed us to share in this great sacrament. In your mercy free us also from all guilt an[d] danger of sin."

11 Cf. Jas 3:2: "For in many things we all offend."

     Cf. 1 Jn 1:8: "If we say that we have no sin, we deceive ourselves, and the truth is not in us." The Council of Carthage comments on this text, as follows: "In regard to the words of the Apostle St. John: 'If we say that we have no sin, we deceive ourselves, and the truth is not in us,' the Council agreed to the following declaration: whoever should hold that this [text] is to be so understood as to mean that it is out of humility that we should say 'we have sin,' and not because this is truly so, let him be anathema" (DS 228).

     Cf. COUNCIL OF TRENT, Session 6 *Decree on Justification*, ch. 11 (DS 1537).

     Cf. SECOND VATICAN COUNCIL, Dogmatic Constitution on the Nature of the Church *Lumen Gentium*, no. 40: "But since we all offend in many things (cf. Jas 3: 2) we all stand in need of God's mercy continuously and must daily pray: 'And forgive us our trespasses' (Mt 6:12)" (AAS 57 [1965] 45).

II.

4. By the hidden and benign mystery of the divine will, a supernatural solidarity reigns among men, whereby the sin of one harms the others just as the holiness of one also benefits the others. Thus the Christian faithful give each other mutual aid to attain their supernatural aim. A testimony of this solidarity is manifested in Adam himself, whose sin is passed on through propagation to all men. But of this supernatural solidarity the greatest and most perfect principle, foundation and example is Christ Himself to communion with Whom God has called us.[12]

5. Indeed Christ "committed no sin,"[13] "suffered for us,"[14] "was wounded for our iniquities, bruised for our sins . . . by His bruises we are healed."[15]

---

12 Cf. AUGUSTINE, *On Baptism, Against the Donatists*, 1, 28: PL 43, 124.
13 Cf. Jn 15:5: "I am the vine, you are the branches. He who abides in me, and I in him, he bears much fruit."
    Cf. 1 Cor 12:27: "Now you are the body of Christ, member for member." Cf. also 1 Cor 1:9, 10:17; Eph 1:20-23.
    Cf. SECOND VATICAN COUNCIL, Dogmatic Constitution on the Nature of the Church *Lumen Gentium*, no. 7 (AAS 57 [1965] 10-11).
    Cf. PIUS XII, Encyclical *Mystici Corporis*: "Through this communication of the Spirit of Christ...the Church becomes the fullness and complement of the Redeemer, Christ being in a certain sense filled out through the Church in all things (see Thomas, *Commentary on the Epistle to the Ephesians*, 1, lesson 8). In these words we arrive at the reason, why . . . the mystical Head, which is Christ, and the Church, which on this earth as another Christ bears his person, are joined together in perpetuating the saving work of the Cross: by Christ we mean the Head and the Body, the Whole Christ" (DS 3813; AAS 35 [1943] 230-231).
    Cf. AUGUSTINE, *Exposition 2 on Psalm 90, 1*: "Our Lord Jesus Christ, as a man complete and perfect, has both head and body. The head we acknowledge to be he who was born of the Virgin Mary. . . . This head is the head of the Church. the body of this head is, not that Church which exists at this time, but that which is made up of the Saints from Abel down to the last men to be born and to believe in Christ, all of them constituting one people and belonging to one city. It is this city which the body, whose head is Christ": CCL 39, p. 1266; PL 37, 1159.
14 Cf. 1 Pt 2:22, 21.
15 Cf. Is 53:4-6 with 1 Pt 2:21-25; cf. also Jn 1:29; Rm 4:25, 5:9ff.; 1 Cor 15:3; 2 Cor 5:21; Gal 1:4; Eph 1:7ff.; Heb 1:3 etc.; 1 Jn 3:5.

Following in the footsteps of Christ,[16] the Christian faithful have always endeavored to help one another on the path leading to the heavenly Father through prayer, the exchange of spiritual goods and penitential expiation. The more they have been immersed in the fervor of charity, the more they have imitated Christ in His sufferings, carrying their crosses in expiation for their own sins and those of others, certain that they could help their brothers to obtain salvation from God the Father of mercies.[17] This is the very ancient dogma of the Communion of

---

16   Cf. 1 Pt 2:21.

17   Cf. Col 1:24: "I rejoice now in the sufferings I bear for your sake; and what is lacking of the sufferings of Christ I fill up in my flesh for his body, which is the Church."

      Cf. CLEMENT OF ALEXANDRIA, *Lib. What rich man shall be saved*, 42: The Apostle St. John exhorts the youthful robber to repentance, exclaiming: "I shall render an account for you to Christ. If it is necessary, I shall willingly suffer death for you, just as the Lord suffered death for us I shall give my life vicariously for yours": GCS *Clement* 3, p. 190; PG 9, 650.

      Cf. CYPRIAN, *On Apostates* 17, 36: "We believe indeed that the merits of the martyrs and the works of the just can avail very much with the judge, when the day of judgment arrives and when this era and world come to an end and the people of Christ are standing before his tribunal." "To him who is repentant, who performs good works, who prays, he can be merciful and forgiving; he can regard as received from them, whatever the martyrs have asked and the priest done on their behalf": CSEL 3l, pp. 249-250, 263; PL 4:495, 508.

      Cf. JEROME, *Against Vigilantius* 6: "You say in your booklet that we can pray one for another while we live, but that no one's prayer for another will be heard after we have died, especially since the martyrs, though crying out for the avenging of their blood, were not able to obtain it (Ap 6: 10). If the apostles and martyrs can pray for others while they are still in the flesh and while they must still have a care for themselves, how much more after they have been crowned, victorious and triumphant?": PL 23, 359.

      Cf. BASIL THE GREAT, *Homily on Julitta*, martyr, 9: "We must therefore weep with those who weep. When you see a brother mourning out of sorrow for his sins, weep with such a man and be sorrowful with him. For the sins of another will thus enable you to correct your own. For he, who sheds fervid tears for the sin of a neighbor, brings healing to himself, at the same time that he weeps for his brother . . . Mourn because of sin. Sin is a sickness of the soul; it brings death to the immortal soul; sin deserves to be mourned and to be lamented with ceaseless weeping": PG 31, 258-259.

      Cf. JOHN CHRYSOSTOM, *Homily on the Epistle to the Philippians* 1, hom. 3, 3: "Let us not, therefore, mourn as a rule those who die, nor let us rejoice

the Saints,[18] whereby the life of each individual son of God in Christ and through Christ is joined by a wonderful link to the life of all his other Christian brothers in the supernatural unity of the Mystical Body of Christ till, as it were, a single mystical person is formed.[19]

---

as a rule over those who live. What then? Let us mourn for sinners, not only when they die, but also while they live. Let us rejoice for the just, not only while they live, but also after they have died": PG 62, 203.

Cf. THOMAS, *S. Th.* 1-2, q. 87, a. 8: "If we speak of that satisfactory punishment, which one takes upon oneself voluntarily, one may bear another's punishment, in so far as they are, in some way, one. . . . If, however, we speak of punishment inflicted on account of sin, inasmuch as it is penal, then each one is punished for his own sin only, because the sinful act is something personal. But if we speak of a punishment that is medicinal, in this way it does happen that one is punished for another's sin. For it has been stated that ills sustained in bodily goods or even in the body itself, are medicinal punishments intended for the health of the soul. Wherefore there is no reason why one should not have suchlike punishments inflicted on one for another's sin, either by God or by man."

18 Cf. LEO XIII, Encyclical *Mirae Caritatis*: "For the Communion of Saints is nothing other . . . than the mutual sharing of help, expiation, prayers and benefits among the faithful who, whether they are already in possession of their heavenly fatherland or are detained in Purgatory or are still living as pilgrims upon earth, are united and form one commonwealth, whose head is Christ, whose form is charity": *Acts of Leo XIII* 22 (1902) 129 (DS 3363).

19 Cf. 1 Cor 12:12-13: "For as the body is one and has many members, and all the members of the body, many as they are, form one body, so also is it with Christ. For in one Spirit we were all baptized into one body."

Cf. PIUS XII, Encyclical *Mystici Corporis*: "In a certain sense [Christ] so lives in the Church that it is as it were another Christ. The doctor of the Gentiles in his letter to the Corinthians affirms this when, without further qualification, he calls the Church 'Christ' (cf. Acts 9:4; 22:7; 26:14). Indeed, if we are to believe Gregory of Nyssa, the Church is often called 'Christ' by the Apostle (cf. *The Life of Moses*: PG 44, 385); and you are conversant, Venerable Brother, with that phrase of Augustine: 'Christ preaches Christ' (cf. Sermons 354, 1; PL 39 1563)" (AAS 35 [1943] 218).

Cf. THOMAS, *S. Th.* 3, q. 48, a. 2 ad 1, and q. 49, a. 1.

Thus is explained the "treasury of the Church"[20] which should certainly not be imagined as the sum total of material goods accumulated in the course of the centuries, but the infinite and inexhaustible value the expiation and the merits of Christ Our Lord have before God, offered as they were so that all of mankind could be set free from sin and attain communion with the Father. It is Christ the Redeemer Himself in whom the satisfactions and merits of His redemption exist and find their force.[21] This treasury also includes the truly immense, unfathomable and ever pristine value before God of the prayers and good works of the Blessed Virgin Mary and all the saints, who following in the footsteps of Christ the Lord and by His grace have sanctified their lives and fulfilled the mission entrusted to them by the Father. Thus while attaining their own salvation, they have also cooperated in the salvation of their brothers in the unity of the Mystical Body.

"For all who are in Christ, having His spirit, form one Church and cleave together in Him" (Eph 4:16). Therefore the union of the wayfarers with the brethren who have gone to sleep in the peace of Christ is not in the least weakened or interrupted, but on the contrary, according to the perpetual faith of

---

20 Cf. CLEMENT VI, Jubilee Bull *Unigenitus Dei Filius*: "The only-begotten Son of God . . . acquired a treasure for the Church militant . . . This treasure . . . he bequeathed to the faithful, to be dispensed for their salvation by the blessed Peter, the keeper of the key of heaven, and by his successors, the vicars of Christ on earth . . . The riches of this treasure, as all acknowledge, are still further increased by the merits of the Blessed Mother of God and by the merits of all the elect from the first just man to the last . . ." (DS 1025, 1026, 1027).

Cf. SIXTUS IV, Encyclical *Romani Pontificis*: "We, to whom the fullness of power has been given from on high, desirous of helping and assisting the souls in Purgatory from the treasury of the universal Church, which is made up of the merits of Christ and of his Saints and which has been entrusted to Us . . ." (DS 1406).

Cf. LEO X, Decree *Cum postquam* to the papal legate Cajetan de Vio: ". . . to dispense the treasure of the merits of Jesus Christ and of the Saints . . ." (DS 1448); cf. DS 1467 and 2641.

21 Cf. Heb 7:23-25, 9:11-28.

the Church, is strengthened by a communication of spiritual goods. For by reason of the fact that those in heaven are more closely united with Christ, they establish the whole Church more firmly in holiness, lend nobility to the worship which the Church offers to God here on earth and in many ways contribute to building it up evermore (1 Cor 12:12-27). For after they have been received into their heavenly home and are present to the Lord (2 Cor 5:8), through Him and with Him and in Him they do not cease to intervene with the Father for us, showing forth the merits which they have won on earth through the one Mediator between God and man, Jesus Christ (1 Tim 2:5), by serving God in all things and filling up in their flesh those things which are lacking of the sufferings of Christ for His Body which is the Church (Col 1:24). Thus by their brotherly interest our weakness is greatly strengthened.[22]

For this reason there certainly exists between the faithful who have already reached their heavenly home, those who are expiating their sins in purgatory and those who are still pilgrims on earth a perennial link of charity and an abundant exchange of all the goods by which, with the expiation of all the sins of the entire Mystical Body, divine justice is placated. God's mercy is thus led to forgiveness, so that sincerely repentant sinners may participate as soon as possible in the full enjoyment of the benefits of the family of God.

---

22 SECOND VATICAN COUNCIL, Dogmatic Constitution on the Nature of the Church *Lumen Gentium*, no. 49 (AAS 57 [1965] 54-55).

III.

6. The Church, aware of these truths ever since its origins, formulated and undertook various ways of applying the fruits of the Lord's redemption to the individual faithful and of leading them to cooperate in the salvation of their brothers, so that the entire body of the Church might be prepared in justice and sanctity for the complete realization of the kingdom of God, when He will be all things to all men.

The Apostles themselves, in fact, exhorted their disciples to pray for the salvation of sinners.[23] This very ancient usage of the Church has blessedly persevered,[24] particularly in the practice of penitents invoking the intercession of the entire community,[25] and when the dead are assisted with suffrages, particularly

---

23   Cf. Jas 5:16: "Confess, therefore, your sins to one another, and pray for one another, that you may be saved. For the unceasing prayer of a just man is of great avail."
     Cf. 1 Jn 5:16: "He who knows his brother is committing a sin that is not unto death, let him ask and life shall be given to him who does not commit a sin unto death."
24   Cf. CLEMENT OF ROME, *To the Corinthians* 56, 1: "Let us also therefore pray for those who are in sin of any kind, that they may be granted the self-mastery and humility to submit, not to us, but to the divine will. For thus the commendation of them to God and the Saints, which is accompanied by mercy, will be fruitful for them and perfect": Funk, *The Apostolic Fathers 1*, 171.
     Cf. *The Martyrdom of St. Polycarp* 8, 1: "But when at last he finished his prayer, in which he made mention of all who at one time or other had been associated with him and who included the small and the great, the famous and the unknown, and the whole Catholic Church throughout the world...": Funk, *The Apostolic Fathers 1*, 321, 323.
25   Cf. SOZOMENUS, *History of the Church* 7, 16: In public penance, after the celebration of Mass, the penitents in the Church of Rome "lamenting and weeping cast themselves prone on the ground. then the Bishop with tears in his eyes comes toward them and prostrates likewise on the ground, the whole assembly of the faithful at the same time weeping and confessing their sins. The Bishop, thereupon, is the first to rise, bids the others to rise also, says an appropriate prayer for the sinners doing penance, and dismisses them": PG 67, 1462.

MANUAL OF INDULGENCES

through the offering of the Eucharistic Sacrifice.[26] Good works, particularly those which human frailty finds difficult, were also offered to God for the salvation of sinners from the Church's most ancient times.[27] And since the sufferings of the martyrs for the faith and for the law of God were considered of great value, penitents used to turn to the martyrs, to be helped by their merits to obtain from the bishops a more speedy reconciliation.[28] Indeed the prayer and good works of the upright were considered to be of so great a value that it could be asserted that the

---

26   Cf. CYRIL OF JERUSALEM, *Catechesis* 23 (mystag. 5) 9; 10: "We then pray also for our deceased holy fathers and bishops, and in general for all among us who departed this life, believing as we do that those souls, for whom prayer is offered, while the sacred and most venerable victim lies before us, will be most greatly helped." After illustrating this by the example of the wreath woven for the emperor that he may grant amnesty to those in exile, the holy Doctor concludes his discourse, saying: "In the same way sinners, do not merely weave a wreath, but we present to God Christ victimized for our sins, striving to obtain from his mercy favor and propitiation both for them and for ourselves": PG 33, 1115, 1118.
      Cf. AUGUSTINE, *Confessions* 9, 12, 32: PL 32, 777; and 9, 11, 27: PL 32, 775; *Sermons* 172, 2: PL 38, 936; *Care to be shown for the Dead* 1, 3; PL 40, 593.

27   Cf. CLEMENT OF ALEXANDRIA, *Lib. What rich man shall be saved* 42: (On the conversion of the young thief by St. John the Apostle) "From then on he spared no effort until—now by frequent prayers to God, now by joining with the young man in protracted fast, now by persuasive and winning words—he succeeded in converting him to the Chruch with firm constancy . . .": CGS 17, pp. 189-190; PG 9, 651.

28   Cf. TERTULLIAN, *To the Martyrs* 1, 6: "Some, not having this peace in the church, were wont to ask for it from the martyrs in prison": CCL 1, p. 3; PL 1, 695.
      Cf. CYPRIAN, *Epistle* 18 (alias: 12) 1: "I think we should come to the aid of our brethren who have received certificates from the martyrs, so that . . ., having received the imposition of hands unto repentance, they may come to the Lord with the peace, which in their letters to us the martyrs have desired to be given to them": CSEL 32, pp. 523-524; PL 4, 265; cf. Epistle 19 [alias: 13], 2, CSEL 32, p, 525; PL 4, 267.
      Cf. EUSEBIUS OF CAESAREA, *History of the Church* 1, 6, 42 CGS Eus. 2, 2, 610; PG 20, 614-615.

penitent was washed, cleansed and redeemed with the help of the entire Christian people.[29]

It was not believed, however, that the individual faithful by their own merits alone worked for the remission of sins of their brothers, but that the entire Church as a single body united to Christ its Head was bringing about satisfaction.[30]

The Church of the Fathers was fully convinced that it was pursuing the work of salvation in community, and under the authority of the pastors established by the Holy Spirit as bishops to govern the Church of God.[31] The bishops, therefore, prudently assessing these matters, established the manner and the measure of the satisfaction to be made and indeed permitted canonical penances to be replaced by other possibly

---

29 Cf. AMBROSE, *On Penance* 1, 15: "for he is cleansed by certain works of the whole people and is washed in the tears of the people, who is redeemed from sin by the prayers and weeping of the people and is cleansed in the inner man. For to his Church, which merited the coming of the Lord Jesus in order that all might be redeemed by one, Christ gave the power to redeem one by means of all": PL 16, 511.

30 Cf. TERTULLIAN, *On Penance* 10 5-6: "The body cannot rejoice when one of its members suffers, but the whole body must needs suffer with it and help to cure it. The Church is in both one and the other; the Church, however, is Christ. When therefore you cast yourself at the knees of your brothers, it is Christ whom you touch, it is Christ whom you implore. In like manner, when they shed tears for you, it is Christ who sorrows, Christ who supplicates the Father. And what the son requests is always easily obtained": CCL 1, p. 337; PL 1, 1356.
    Cf. AUGUSTINE, *Exposition on Ps 85, 1*: CCL 39, p. 1176-1177; PL 37, 1082.

31 Cf. Acts 20:28. Also cf. COUNCIL OF TRENT, Session 23, Decr. *On the Sacrament of Orders*, ch. 4 (DS 1768); FIRST VATICAN COUNCIL, Session 4, Dogmatic Constitution on the Church *Pastor Aeternus*, ch. 3 (DS 3061); SECOND VATICAN COUNCIL, Dogmatic Constitution on the Church *Lumen Gentium*, no. 20 (AAS 57 [1965] 23).
    Cf. IGNATIUS OF ANTIOCH, *To the Church of Smyrna* 8, 1: "Apart from the Bishop, let no one perform any of the functions that pertain to the Church . . ." Funk, *The Apostolic Fathers 1*, p. 283.

easier works, which would be useful to the common good and suitable for fostering piety, to be performed by the penitents themselves and sometimes by others among the faithful.[32]

IV.

7. The conviction existing in the Church that the pastors of the flock of the Lord could set the individual free from the vestiges of sins by applying the merits of Christ and of the saints led gradually, in the course of the centuries and under the influence of the Holy Spirit's continuous inspiration of the people of God, to the usage of indulgences which represented a progression in the doctrine and discipline of the Church rather than a change.[33] From the roots of revelation a new advantage grew in benefit to the faithful and the entire Church.

The use of indulgences, which spread gradually, became a very evident fact in the history of the Church when the

---

32 Cf. First Council of Nicea, can. 12: "those who by their reverence, tears, patience and good works show that in their conduct and disposition they have really been converted can, after having spent the required period of time as 'hearers' be admitted to join the faithful in prayer, saving the right of the Bishop to treat them with greater leniency . . .": Mansi, SS. Conciliorum collectio 2, 674.

Cf. Council of Neocaesarea, can. 3, loc. cit. 540.

Cf. Innocent I, Epistle 25, 7, 10: PL 20, 559.

Cf. Leo the Great, Epistle 159, 6: PL 54, 1138.

Cf. Basil the Great, Epistle 217 (canonica 3) 74: "Yet if any of those who have fallen into the above-mentioned sins should show himself earnest in doing penance, he who by God's mercy has been given the power to loose and to bind will not be deserving of censure if, because of the extraordinary penance already performed by the sinner, he should exercise clemency and shorten the time of the penance. For, what is narrated in the Scriptures teaches us that those who give themselves with greater intensity to penance quickly receive the mercy of God": PG 32, 803.

Cf. Ambrose, On Penance 1, 15 (see above, in note 29).

33 Cf. Vincent of Lerins, Commonitorium primum 23: PL 50, 667-668.

Roman Pontiffs decreed that certain works useful to the common good of the Church "could replace all penitential practices"[34] and that the faithful who were "truly repentant and had confessed their sins" and performed such works were granted "by the mercy of Almighty God and . . . trusting in the merits and the authority of His Apostles" and 'by virtue of the fullness of the apostolic power,' not only full and abundant forgiveness, but the most complete forgiveness for their sins possible."[35]

For "the only-begotten son of God . . . has won a treasure for the militant Church . . . and has entrusted it to blessed Peter, the keybearer of heaven, and to his successors, Christ's vicars on earth, that they may distribute it to the faithful for their salvation, applying it mercifully for reasonable causes to all who are repentant and have confessed their sins, at times remitting completely and at times partially the temporal punishment due sin in a general as well as in special ways insofar as they judge it to be fitting in the eyes of the Lord. It is known that the merits of the Blessed Mother of God and of all the elect . . . add further to this treasure."[36]

---

34 Cf. COUNCIL OF CLAREMONT, can. 2: "If anyone, moved solely by devotion to the exclusion of any desire for renown or riches, shall set out to liberate the Church of God in Jerusalem, that journey shall be accounted as satisfaction for every penance": Mansi, *SS. Conciliorum collectio* 20, 816.

35 Cf. BONIFACE VIII, Bull *Antiquorum habet*: "We have it on the trustworthy testimony of very early writers, that liberal remissions and indulgences for sins were granted to those who visited the venerable basilica of the Prince of the Apostles in Rome. We therefore, . . . holding these remissions and indulgences to be singly and collectively valid and pleasing, confirm and approve them by virtue of the Apostolic authority . . . Trusting in the mercy of Almighty God and in the merits and authority of the same Apostles and after consultation with our brothers, we by virtues of the fullness of the Apostolic authority do now for this centennial year and will in the future for each recurring centennial year grant, not only a full and more abundant, but the fullest pardon of sins to those who, truly repentant and having confessed their sins, devoutly visit these basilicas . . ." (DS 868).

36 CLEMENT VI, Jubilee Bull *Unigenitus Dei Filius* (DS 1025, 1026, 1027).

8. The remission of the temporal punishment due for sins already forgiven insofar as their guilt is concerned has been called specifically "indulgence."[37]

It has something in common with other ways or means of eliminating the vestiges of sin but at the same time it is clearly distinct from them.

In an indulgence in fact, the Church, making use of its power as minister of the Redemption of Christ, not only prays but by an authoritative intervention dispenses to the faithful suitably disposed the treasury of satisfaction which Christ and the saints won for the remission of temporal punishment.[38]

---

37 Cf. LEO X, Decree *Cum postquam*: "We have considered it our duty to make clear to you, that the Church of Rome, which all others are obliged to follow as their Mother, has traditionally taught, that the Roman Pontiff, as the successor of Peter the Bearer of the Keys and as the Vicar of Christ Jesus on earth, can for a reasonable cause grant from the superabundance of the merits of Christ and the Saints indulgences in favor of those of the faithful who, whether in this life or in purgatory, are members of Christ, joined to him in charity; this he can do by virtue of the power of the keys, the power namely to open the kingdom of heaven by freeing the faithful from impediments that bar them from it (from the impediment of guilt for their actual sins by the Sacrament of Penance and from the impediment of temporal punishment due in divine justice for these sins by ecclesiastical indulgence). It is also the tradition of the Church that, in granting by Apostolic authority an indulgence whether for the living or the dead, the Roman Pontiff dispenses the treasury of the merits of Christ and the Saints and that it was his wont to grant an indulgence (for the living) after the manner of an absolution and (for the dead) to transfer it in the form of a suffrage. Therefore all, both living and dead, who truly gain an indulgence, are freed from as much of the temporal punishment due in divine justice for their sins, as is granted by the indulgence acquired" (DS 1447-1448).

38 Cf. PAUL VI, Letter *Sacrosancta Portiunculae*: "An indulgence, which the Church grants to the penitent, is a manifestation of that marvelous Communion of Saints, which by the single bond of the charity of Christ mystically unites the Most Blessed Virgin Mary and the company of the faithful, whether triumphant in heaven or detained in purgatory or still living as pilgrims upon earth. For an indulgence, given by the intervention of the Church, lessens or entirely remits the punishment, by which a person is in a certain sense prevented from attaining a closer union with God. The repentant, therefore, will find in this unique form of ecclesial charity an ever available help in putting off the old man and putting on the new, 'who is being renewed unto perfect knowledge according to the image of his Creator' (Col 3:10)" (AAS 58 [1966] 663-634).

The aim pursued by ecclesiastical authority in granting indulgences is not only that of helping the faithful to expiate the punishment due sin but also that of urging them to perform works of piety, penitence and charity—particularly those which lead to growth in faith and which favor the common good.[39]

And if the faithful offer indulgences in suffrage for the dead, they cultivate charity in an excellent way and while raising their minds to heaven, they bring a wiser order into the things of this world.

The Magisterium of the Church has defended and illustrated this doctrine in various documents.[40] Unfortunately, the

---

39 Cf. PAUL VI, cited Letter: "As for those of the faithful who are repentant and strive to attain to this 'metanoia,' the Church comes to their help, for the reason that, having sinned, they now aspire to that holiness, with which they were clothed in Baptism. By grants of indulgences, she enfolds these her children in a maternal embrace, helping and sustaining them in their weakness and frailty. An indulgence, therefore, is not some easy way, by which we can escape the necessity of doing penance for sin. It is rather a support, which each of the faithful, humbly conscious of his weakness, finds in the mystical Body of Christ, 'collaborating in its entirety by charity, example and prayers to effect his conversion' (Dogmatic constitution on the Church, no. 11)" (AAS 58 [1966] 632).

40 CLEMENT VI, Jubilee Bull *Unigenitus Dei Filius* (DS 1026).
    CLEMENT VI, Letter *Super quibusdam* (DS 1059).
    MARTIN V, Bull *Inter cunctas* (DS 1266). SIXTUS IV, Bull *Salvator noster* (DS 1398). SIXTUS IV, Encyclical *Romani Pontificis provida*: "Desiring to counteract by Our Briefs . . . these scandals and errors, We have written to . . . prelates to notify the faithful that the plenary indulgence for the souls in purgatory was granted by Us after the manner of a suffrage, not in order that the faithful might be deterred by this indulgence from performing pious and good works, but in order that the indulgence might be of salutary benefit to the souls (in purgatory) after the manner of a suffrage and profit them, just as would devout prayers and pious alms said and offered for the welfare of these souls . . . It was not that We intended to say, nor do We now intend to say or wish to imply, that an indulgence is of no more benefit or value than alms or prayers or that alms and prayers are of equal benefit or value as an indulgence after the manner of suffrage; for, We know that there is a great difference between alms and prayers on the one hand and an indulgence after the manner of a suffrage on the other; but We said that an indulgence (after the manner of a suffrage) avails (the souls in purgatory) just as ('*perinde ac si*') do prayers and alms, that is, 'in the same manner.' And because

practice of indulgences has at times been improperly used either through "untimely and superfluous indulgences" by which the power of the keys was humiliated and penitential satisfaction weakened,[41] or through the collection of "illicit

---

prayers and alms have a suffrage-value when performed for the souls in purgatory, We, to whom the fullness of power has been given by God, desiring to assist the souls in purgatory with suffrages from the treasury of the universal Church—a treasury made up of the merits of Christ and the Saints and committed to Us—have granted the above-mentioned indulgence . . ." (DS 1405-1406).

LEO X, Bull *Exsurge Domine* (DS 1467-1472).

PIUS VI, Constitution *Auctorem fidei*, proposition 40: "The proposition is false, rash, injurious to the merits of Christ, and long since condemned in article 19 of Luther, which asserts, 'that according to its precise meaning an indulgence is nothing more than the remission of part of that penance to which a sinner is obliged according to the stipulations of the canons,' as though an indulgence, apart from the mere remission of a canonical penalty, does not also effect the remission of the temporal punishment due the divine justice for actual sins" (DS 2640). Ibid., proposition 41: "Likewise false, rash injurious to the merits of Christ and the Saints, and long since condemned in article 17 of Luther is the statement subjoined to the above proposition, 'that the scholastics, puffed up by their subtleties, introduced an erroneous understanding of the treasury of the merits of Christ and the Saints, and in place of the clear notion of absolution from a canonical penalty substituted the confused and false notion of applying these merits,' as though the treasurers of the Church, on which the Pope draws in granting indulgences, were not the merits of Christ and the Saints" (DS 2641). Ibid., proposition 42: "Likewise false, rash offensive to pious ears, injurious to the Roman Pontiffs and to the practice and understanding of the universal Church, leading to the condemned heretical error of Peter of Osma, and condemned also in article 22 of Luther is the statement added to the above proposition, 'that it is still more to be regretted that it was decided to transfer this fanciful application (of merits) to the departed'" (DS 2642).

PIUS XI, Proclamation of the Extraordinary Holy Year *Quod nuper*: "We grant and impart mercifully in the Lord the fullest remission of the entire debt of punishment which they owe in atonement for their sins, provided they have first obtained the remission and pardon of the sins themselves" (AAS 25 [1933] 8).

PIUS XII, Proclamation of the Universal Jubilee *Jubilaeum maximum*: "To all the faithful who in the course of this year of atonement, having duly received the Sacraments of Penance and Holy Communion, devoutly visit the Basilicas and recite . . . prayers . . ., we grant and impart mercifully in the Lord the fullest remission of the entire debt of punishment which they owe in expiation for their sins" (AAS 41 [1949] 258-259).

41 Cf. FOURTH LATERAN COUNCIL, ch. 62 (DS 819).

profits" by which indulgences were blasphemously defamed.[42] But the Church, in deploring and correcting these improper uses "teaches and establishes that the use of indulgences must be preserved because it is supremely salutary for the Christian people and authoritatively approved by the sacred councils; and it condemns with anathema those who maintain the uselessness of indulgences or deny the power of the Church to grant them."[43]

9. The Church also in our days then invites all its sons to ponder and meditate well on how the use of indulgences benefits their lives and indeed all Christian society.

To recall briefly the most important considerations, this salutary practice teaches us in the first place how it is "sad and bitter to have abandoned . . . the Lord God."[44] Indeed the faithful when they acquire indulgences understand that by their own powers they could not remedy the harm they have done to themselves and to the entire community by their sin, and they are therefore stirred to a salutary humility.

Furthermore, the use of indulgences shows us how closely we are united to each other in Christ, and how the supernatural life of each can benefit others so that these also may be more easily and more closely united with the Father. Therefore the use of indulgences effectively influences charity in us and demonstrates that charity in an outstanding manner when we offer indulgences as assistance to our brothers who rest in Christ.

10. Likewise, the religious practice of indulgences reawakens trust and hope in a full reconciliation with God the Father, but

---

42   Cf. COUNCIL OF TRENT, Decr. *On Indulgences* (DS 1835).
43   Cf. ibid.
44   Jer 2:19.

in such a way as will not justify any negligence nor in any way diminish the effort to acquire the dispositions required for full communion with God. Although indulgences are in fact free gifts, nevertheless they are granted for the living as well as for the dead only on determined conditions. To acquire them, it is indeed required on the one hand that prescribed works be performed, and on the other that the faithful have the necessary dispositions, that is to say, that they love God, detest sin, place their trust in the merits of Christ and believe firmly in the great assistance they derive from the Communion of Saints.

In addition, it should not be forgotten that by acquiring indulgences the faithful submit docilely to the legitimate pastors of the Church and above all to the successor of Blessed Peter, the keybearer of heaven, to whom the Savior Himself entrusted the task of feeding His flock and governing His Church.

The salutary institution of indulgences therefore contributes in its own way to bringing it about that the Church appear before Christ without blemish or defect, but holy and immaculate,[45] admirably united with Christ in the supernatural bond of charity. Since in fact by means of indulgences members of the Church who are undergoing purification are united more speedily to those of the Church in heaven, the kingdom of Christ is through these same indulgences established more extensively and more speedily "until we all attain to the unity of the faith and of the deep knowledge of the Son of God, to perfect manhood, to the mature measure of the fullness of Christ."[46]

11. Therefore Holy Mother Church, supported by these truths, while again recommending to the faithful the practice of indulgences as something very dear to the Christian people

45   Cf. Eph 5:27.
46   Eph 4:13.

during the course of many centuries and in our days as well—this is proven by experience—does not in any way intend to diminish the value of other means of sanctification and purification, first and foremost among which are the Sacrifice of the Mass and the Sacraments, particularly the Sacrament of Penance. Nor does it diminish the importance of those abundant aids which are called sacramentals or of the works of piety, penitence and charity. All these aids have this in common that they bring about sanctification and purification all the more efficaciously, the more closely the faithful are united with Christ the Head and the Body of the Church by charity. The preeminence of charity in the Christian life is confirmed also by indulgences. For indulgences cannot be acquired without a sincere conversion of mentality ("metanoia") and unity with God, to which the performance of the prescribed works is added. Thus the order of charity is preserved, into which is incorporated the remission of punishment by distribution from the Church's treasury.

While recommending that its faithful not abandon or neglect the holy traditions of their forebears but welcome them religiously as a precious treasure of the Catholic family and duly esteem them, the Church nevertheless leaves it to each to use these means of purification and sanctification with the holy and free liberty of the sons of God. It constantly reminds them, though, of those things which are to be given preference because they are necessary or at least better and more efficacious for the attainment of salvation.[47]

---

47 Cf. Thomas, *Commentary on the fourth book of the Sentences*, dist. 20, q. I, a. 3, q. la 2, ad 2 (S. Th. Suppl., q. 25, a. 2, ad 2): "although such indulgences are of great value for the remission of temporal punishment, still other works of satisfaction are more meritorious from the standpoint of the essential reward; this is infinitely better than the remission of temporal punishment."

Holy Mother Church has then deemed it fitting, in order to give greater dignity and esteem to the use of indulgences, to introduce some innovations into its discipline of indulgences and has accordingly ordered the issuance of new norms.

V.

12. The following norms introduce appropriate variations in the discipline of indulgences, taking into consideration the proposals advanced by the episcopal conferences.

The rulings of the *Code of Canon Law* and of the decrees of the Holy See concerning indulgences which do not go counter to the new norms remain unchanged.

In drawing up the new norms these three considerations have been particularly observed: to establish a new measurement for partial indulgences; to reduce considerably the number of plenary indulgences; and, as for the so-called "real" and "local" indulgences, to reduce them and give them a simpler and more dignified formulation.

Regarding partial indulgences, with the abolishment of the former determination of days and years, a new norm or measurement has been established which takes into consideration the action itself of the faithful Christian who performs a work to which an indulgence is attached.

Since by their acts the faithful can obtain, in addition to the merit which is the principal fruit of the act, a further remission of temporal punishment in proportion to the degree to which the charity of the one performing the act is greater, and in proportion to the degree to which the act itself is performed in a more perfect way, it has been considered fitting that this remission of temporal punishment which the Christian faithful acquire through an action should serve as the measurement for the remission of punishment which the ecclesiastical authority bountifully adds by way of partial indulgence.

It has also been considered fitting to reduce appropriately the number of plenary indulgences in order that the faithful may hold them in greater esteem and may in fact acquire them with the proper dispositions. For indeed the greater the proliferation (of indulgences) the less is the attention given them; what is offered in abundance is not greatly appreciated. Besides, many of the faithful need considerable time to prepare themselves properly for the acquisition of a plenary indulgence.

As regards the "real" and "local" indulgences, not only has their number been reduced considerably, but the designations themselves have been abolished to make it clearer that indulgences are attached to the actions performed by the faithful and not to objects or places which are but the occasion for the acquisition of the indulgences. In fact, members of pious associations can acquire the indulgences proper to their associations without the requirement of the use of distinctive objects.

Norms*

N1. An indulgence is the remission before God of the temporal punishment due sins already forgiven as far as their guilt is concerned, which the follower of Christ with the proper dispositions and under certain determined conditions acquires through the intervention of the Church which, as minister of the Redemption, authoritatively dispenses and applies the treasury of the satisfaction won by Christ and the saints.

N2. An indulgence is partial or plenary according as it removes either part or all of the temporal punishment due sin.

N3. Partial as well as plenary indulgences can always be applied to the dead by way of suffrage.

N4. A partial indulgence will henceforth be designated only with the words "partial indulgence" without any determination of days or years.

N5. The faithful who at least with a contrite heart perform an action to which a partial indulgence is attached obtain, in addition to the remission of temporal punishment acquired by the action itself, an equal remission of punishment through the intervention of the Church.

N6. A plenary indulgence can be acquired only once a day, except for the provisions contained in N18 for those who are on the point of death. A partial indulgence can be acquired

---

*   This set of norms is part of Pope Paul VI's apostolic constitution *Indulgentiarum doctrina* and is provided for historical study only. The norms currently in effect for indulgences begin on pp. 11-20 of this book.

more than once a day, unless there is an explicit indication to the contrary.

N7.   To acquire a plenary indulgence it is necessary to perform the work to which the indulgence is attached and to fulfill three conditions: sacramental confession, Eucharistic Communion and prayer for the intentions of the Supreme Pontiff. It is further required that all attachment to sin, even to venial sin, be absent. If this disposition is in any way less than complete, or if the prescribed three conditions are not fulfilled, the indulgence will be only partial, except for the provisions contained in N11 for those who are "impeded."

N8.   The three conditions may be fulfilled several days before or after the performance of the prescribed work; nevertheless it is fitting that Communion be received and the prayers for the intentions of the Supreme Pontiff be said the same day the work is performed.

N9.   A single sacramental confession suffices for gaining several plenary indulgences, but Communion must be received and prayers for the Supreme Pontiff's intentions recited for the gaining of each plenary indulgence.

N10.   The condition of praying for the Supreme Pontiff's intentions is fully satisfied by reciting one "Our Father" and one "Hail Mary"; nevertheless the individual faithful are free to recite any other prayer according to their own piety and devotion toward the Supreme Pontiff.

N11.   While there is no change in the faculty granted by canon 935 of the *Code of Canon Law* to confessors to commute for those who are "impeded" either the prescribed work itself or the required conditions [for the acquisition of indulgences], local Ordinaries can grant to the faithful over whom they exercise authority in accordance with the law, and who live in places where it is impossible or at least very difficult for them to receive the sacraments of confession and Communion, permission to acquire a plenary indulgence without confession and Communion provided they are sorry for their sins and have the intention of receiving these sacraments as soon as possible.

N12. The division of indulgences into "personal," "real" and "local" is abolished so as to make it clearer that indulgences are attached to the actions of the faithful even though at times they may be linked with some object or place.

N13. The *Enchiridion Indulgentiarium* (collection of indulgenced prayers and works) is to be revised with a view to attaching indulgences only to the most important prayers and works of piety, charity and penance.

N14. The lists and summaries of indulgences special to religious orders, congregations, societies of those living in community without vows, secular institutes and the pious associations of faithful are to be revised as soon as possible in such a way that plenary indulgences may be acquired only on particular days established by the Holy See acting on the recommendation of the Superior General, or in the case of pious associations, of the local Ordinary.

N15. A plenary indulgence applicable only to the dead can be acquired in all churches and public oratories—and in semipublic oratories by those who have the right to use them—on November 2.

In addition, a plenary indulgence can be acquired twice a year in parish churches: on the feast of the church's titular saint and on August 2, when the "Portiuncula" occurs, or on some other more opportune day determined by the Ordinary.

All the indulgences mentioned above can be acquired either on the days established or—with the consent of the Ordinary—on the preceding or the following Sunday.

Other indulgences attached to churches and oratories are to be revised as soon as possible.

N16. The work prescribed for acquiring a plenary indulgence connected with a church or oratory consists in a devout visit and the recitation of an "Our Father" and "Creed."

N17. The faithful who use with devotion an object of piety (crucifix, cross, rosary, scapular or medal) properly blessed by any priest, can acquire a partial indulgence.

But if this object of piety is blessed by the Supreme Pontiff or any bishop, the faithful who use it devoutly can also acquire a plenary indulgence on the feast of the holy Apostles Peter and Paul, provided they also make a profession of faith using any legitimate formula.

N18. To the faithful in danger of death who cannot be assisted by a priest to bring them the sacraments and impart the apostolic blessing with its attendant plenary indulgence (according to canon 468 §2 of the *Code of Canon Law*) Holy Mother Church nevertheless grants a plenary indulgence to be acquired at the point of death, provided they are properly disposed and have been in the habit of reciting some prayers during their lifetime. To use a crucifix or cross in connection with the acquisition of this plenary indulgence is a laudable practice.

This plenary indulgence at the point of death can be acquired by the faithful even if they have already obtained another plenary indulgence on the same day.

N19. The norms established regarding plenary indulgences, particularly those referred to in N16, apply also to what up to now have been known as the "toties quoties" ("as often as") plenary indulgences.

N20. Holy Mother Church, extremely solicitous for the faithful departed, has decided that suffrages can be applied to them to the widest possible extent at any Sacrifice of the Mass whatsoever, abolishing all special privileges in this regard.

These new norms regulating the acquisition of indulgences will go into effect three months from the date of publication of this constitution in the *Acta Apostolicae Sedis*.

Indulgences attached to the use of religious objects which are not mentioned above cease three months after the date of publication of this constitution in the *Acta Apostolicae Sedis*.

The revisions mentioned in N14 and N15 must be submitted to the Sacred Apostolic Penitentiary within a year. Two years after the date of this constitution, indulgences which have not been confirmed will become null and void.

We will that these statutes and prescriptions of ours be established now and remain in force for the future notwithstanding, if it is necessary so to state, the constitutions and apostolic directives published by our predecessors or any other prescriptions even if they might be worthy of special mention or should otherwise require partial repeal.

Given at Rome at St. Peter's on January 1, the octave of the Nativity of Our Lord Jesus Christ, 1967, the fourth year of Our Pontificate.

POPE PAUL VI

INDICES

A. PRAYERS

B. PLENARY INDULGENCES

C. GENERAL INDEX

ADDITIONAL RESOURCES

Pastoral Care of the Dying
Pastoral Care of the Dying provides a convenient resource of the
official texts of the Church for those at the bed side of Catholics
in their final hours. Sections include the Commendation of the
Dying, Celebration of Viaticum Outside Mass, and Prayers for the
Dead. Care of a dying child is also discussed.
No. 5-487, 78 pp.

Night Prayer
From the Liturgy of the Hours
This volume, drawn from the *Liturgy of the Hours*, offers the last
prayer of the day, from Monday to Sunday, together with hymns
and psalmody, scripture readings and gospel canticles, said before
going to bed, no matter the time.
No. 5-148, 80 pp.

Compendium of the Catechism of the Catholic Church
This 200-page volume in question-and-answer format offers a
quick synopsis of the essential contents of the faith as promul-
gated in the Catechism of the Catholic Church. Also included is
an appendix with common prayers in the vernacular and Latin.
English
Hardcover: No. 5-725, 200 pp.
Paperback: No. 5-720, 200 pp.

Spanish
Hardcover: No. 5-921, 225 pp.
Paperback: No. 5-920, 225 pp.

For information on our selection of prayer cards for a variety of
important occasions, to go *www.usccbpublishing.org*.